International Chinese Language Education Development Report

2019-2020

Compiler-in-Chief: Liu Li
Deputy Compiler-in-Chief: Chen Lixia

北京语言大学出版社
BEIJING LANGUAGE AND CULTURE UNIVERSITY PRESS

Preface

Language is an important tool for human communication, and language communication and cooperation are the essential needs of the common development and progress of human society. Based on a brief review and prospect of international Chinese language education, this report will focus on the basic components of international Chinese language education, such as current research, teacher training, textbook construction, Chinese proficiency testing, Confucius Institutes, etc. The development of international Chinese language education in typical regions will be introduced, and the research on teaching and learning Chinese as a second language will be the special focus of 2019–2020.

I. Keynote

The report provides an all-round review of international Chinese language education with both confidence and introspection. It comprehensively and objectively reflects and evaluates the development of international Chinese language education in a scientific approach, summing up the achievements in a practical way, and gives positive recognition to the achievements of international Chinese language education; in the meanwhile, the report confronts the existing problems head-on and clearly defines our efforts in the future instead of sidestepping challenges, thus providing an important reference for the transformation, upgrading, and high-quality development of international Chinese language teaching.

II. Value

Based on the new situation of international Chinese language education development in 2019–2020, this report grasps the theme of creating a new model of international

Chinese language education, and expounds the development process, actual achievements, and future trends of international Chinese language education in view of the realistic needs of its transformation and upgrading.

The publication of the report will be helpful to comprehensively understand the development of international Chinese language education at home and abroad, promote the research and practice of international Chinese language education in the new era, scientifically learn the specific process of international Chinese language teaching, and objectively evaluate the achievements of international Chinese language education reform. Promoting international Chinese language education research in the form of annual reports is an inherent demand and a major milestone for the development and reform of international Chinese language education.

III. Features

Based on the reality and with the wisdom of foreign and domestic experts and scholars, the report strives to reflect the following features:

(1) Promptly reflect development trends

The report aims to accurately reflect the development and overall situation of international Chinese language education, and objectively show the research results in this area. On the basis of a macro understanding of the current situations of international Chinese language teaching, the report tries to present the prominent problems faced by international Chinese language education and puts forward practical suggestions.

(2) Emphasize the awareness of problem-solving

The report actively responds to different concerns about international Chinese language education from all walks of life in China and from the international community, and provides responses and references for the stakeholders engaged in and concerned about international Chinese language education. The report unfolds multiple dimensions, focuses on a comprehensive review of the main achievements in the development of international Chinese language education in 2019-2020, and systematically presents the development overview and the main achievements in this field with concise comments.

(3) Make scientific analysis and judgment

The sustainable development of international Chinese language education is inseparable from the basic theoretical support of the discipline. In addition to objectively presenting the latest development trend of international Chinese language education, the report also conducts an in-depth analysis of the teachers, textbooks and teaching methods of international Chinese language teaching. It describes the development experience and the illuminations of international Chinese language teaching, and analyzes and predicts its environment and challenges in the new era as well as the future development trend.

According to the report, international Chinese language education boasts distinct characteristics which are not possessed by general disciplines in terms of internal and external environment, service targets, and knowledge systems, thus requiring special attention. The discipline construction of international Chinese language education has become increasingly mature in recent years, which has further promoted the development of international Chinese language teaching. Meanwhile, concerning the discipline, there are still many theoretical and practical problems to be solved.

(4) Unite domestic and overseas intellectual resources

The author team members of the report are from a wide range of fields, including domestic experts and scholars who have long been engaged in and studied international Chinese language teaching, as well as renowned overseas scholars and Sinologists. In addition to Chinese, the report will be published in a variety of languages (English, French, Spanish, Arabic and Russian) to further promote dialogue with the international education community.

International Chinese Language Education Development Report 2019–2020 hopes to play a positive role in facilitating mutual learning among diverse civilizations, further promoting the sustainable and high-quality development of international Chinese language education, and advancing language and cultural exchanges and cooperation between China and other countries in the world. At the same time, we will make efforts to build a professional collaboration platform for international Chinese language education research on the basis of the report so as to serve the connotative and innovative high-quality development of international Chinese language education. We hope this annual report will inspire us to advance the construction of a big data platform and facilitate the innovation and development of international Chinese language education to build a more open, inclusive and standardized international Chinese language education system.

Contents

I Comprehensive Report

Development History, Current Situation and Prospect of International Chinese Language Education

Taking international Chinese language education in 2019 as a transversal report and the longitudinal review of the development history and future prospects of international Chinese language education as another dimension, this chapter provides a three-dimensional depiction and analysis of international Chinese language education development from the perspectives of time and space against the global background of international Chinese language education.

I. Development History

Language is the bridge of human communication, and language education is the best way to realize effective human communication. In the nearly 70 years since the founding of the People's Republic of China, international Chinese language education has always been focused on Chinese language teaching, making its orientation and direction clear from the very beginning. In 1950, Special Chinese Language Course for the Exchange Students from Eastern Europe was established at Tsinghua University, starting the prelude to international Chinese language education in the People's Republic of China. The Special Course, which can be said to be the first international Chinese education agency in the PRC, was headed by Mr. Zhou Peiyuan, the famous physicist and Dean of Tsinghua University at that time. What's more, the textbook used was an adapted version of Yuen Ren Chao's *Mandarin Primer*. Since then, the Special Course has gone through stages of Special Chinese Language Course for Foreign Students at Peking University, the BFSU Overseas Students Affairs Office and the Higher Preparatory School for Foreign Students. Finally, it evolved to be Beijing Language Institute in 1964. In 1952, the PRC sent Zhu Dexi abroad as the first teacher to participate in the overseas Chinese language teaching. In 1961, 25 fresh college graduates from Chinese language departments were selected from 10 universities and sent abroad as the first batch of Chinese language teachers. It can be said that international Chinese language education initiated as a national cause in the 1950s and 1960s and started from a high level in terms of teacher selection and textbook selection as most of the international Chinese language teachers of that time later became famous language teaching experts and linguists.

Since the reform and opening up in 1978, international Chinese language education has entered a period of great development. It has made historic breakthroughs from a national cause to an academic discipline such as in Chinese language talents education and training. In 1978, Lyu Bisong first proposed that Chinese language teaching for foreigners should be developed as a separate discipline, and a major program for teacher training should be established in Chinese colleges and universities, and specialized research institutions should be set up. The year of 1983 witnessed the establishment of Duiwai Hanyu Teaching & Research Association affiliated with Chinese Society of Education and "Teaching Chinese as a Foreign Language (TCFL)" as a separate discipline was formally created. In that year, Beijing Language Institute began to recruit undergraduate students, and in 1986, postgraduate students were enrolled. In 1997, doctoral students, whose research direction is Teaching Chinese as a Foreign Language, were recruited under the subject catalogue of "Linguistics and Applied Linguistics". In 1987, China National Office for Teaching Chinese as a Foreign Language (Hanban) was established. The International Society for Chinese Language Teaching was founded and held its first conference in the same year; in June of 1990, the Ministry of Education of the People's Republic of China promulgated *Measures for Certifying Teachers' Ability to Teach Chinese as a Foreign Language*. Thanks to continuous efforts, the orientation and functions of the discipline of international Chinese language education have been consistently improved, the cultivation of talents has become specialized and professionalized, the academic research results based on international Chinese language education have a growing influence, and the discipline construction system has become more mature and systematic. If international Chinese language education is said to start as a national cause, then by the 1980s and 1990s, it had been motivated to develop as both a cause and a discipline.

Entering the 21st century, with continuous enhancement of China's national strength, the economic prosperity stimulated the "Chinese fever" around the world. The ever-increasing demand of overseas Chinese language learners to come to China to learn Chinese can hardly be met. As a result, the demand for setting up Chinese teaching institutions in the local countries has also sharply increased. Therefore, under the guidance of Hanban, Confucius Institutes have been established in succession in many countries since 2004. By December 2019, a total of 550 Confucius Institutes and 1,172 Confucius Classrooms have been established in 162 countries (regions) around the world. In 2005, the opening of World Chinese Language Conference marked the gradual transformation of the international Chinese language education discipline from Teaching Chinese as a Foreign Language to International Chinese Language Education. In 2011, the Ministry of Education issued *The Directory of Degree Awarding and Personnel Training*, and TCFL was officially renamed as Teaching Chinese to Speakers of Other Languages (TCSOL). Meanwhile, a number of colleges and universities have established TCSOL Master's and Doctor's degree programs.

With the theme of "Innovation and Development of International Chinese Language Education in the New Era", 2019 International Chinese Language Education Conference marked a new period for TCSOL development. In the future, the international Chinese language education should focus on integrating into the local community abroad, accommodating the needs of the other party. Meanwhile, the transformation and upgrading of international Chinese language education should be realized by promoting the "Chinese + vocational skills" program, improving the evaluation standards of international Chinese language education, and promoting the diversification of school subjects.

Looking back at the history of international Chinese language education, it can be broadly divided into four stages: the first stage (1950-1982) is the start-up period when the discipline was not formed yet during the early phase of the PRC; the second stage (1983-2004) is the formation period of the discipline. International Chinese language education became a specialized discipline in the name of "Teaching Chinese as a Foreign Language" and gradually developed a complete teaching theory system; the third stage (2005-2018) is the exploration and development period. During this period, Confucius Institutes landed overseas, which was an important exploration for international Chinese language education to "go global"; TCFL has transformed into TCSOL, which has achieved leapfrog development as both a cause and a discipline. The fourth stage (2019-now) is the period of transition and upgrading. Against the backdrop of the new era, in the face of the diversified demands for Chinese language learning worldwide and the tremendous challenges faced by Confucius Institutes, international Chinese language education will further improve its quality and efficiency, adapt to the new situation and new changes, and explore new development models.

II. Current Situation

2019 witnessed an eventful year for international Chinese language education, when international Chinese language education continued the themes of development and inheritance, promoted innovation of disciplines, actively explored ways of transformation and upgradations, and made remarkable achievements in system construction, talents training, exchanges and cooperation. It was also in 2019, the idea of building a community with a shared future for mankind was deeply rooted in the hearts of the people, and the "Belt and Road" Initiative was in full swing, which requires a large number of interdisciplinary talents who can speak Chinese and master certain technology. The great market demand has also impelled Chinese language teaching to explore the teaching model of "Chinese + vocational skills" in addition to the cultivation of general language communication abilities.

1. System Construction

In 2019, international Chinese language education and Confucius Institutes continued to establish and improve relevant systems:

(1) The opinion solicitation meeting for *Chinese Language Test Management Measures* was held at the University of Chinese Academy of Sciences in Beijing, and 38 excellent responsible officers of tests at home and abroad participated.

(2) The research project was approved for the revision of the *Standards for Teachers of Chinese to Speakers of Other Languages* and the development of the graded competence certification.

(3) The *Standards for Confucius Institutes' School Running* and the *Index System of Standards for Appraising Confucius Institutes' Performance in School Running* were formulated based on extensive consultations.

2. Institution Building

By December 2019, 550 Confucius Institutes and 1,172 Confucius Classrooms in primary and secondary schools have been set up in 162 countries (regions). Among them, 27 Confucius Institutes and 66 Confucius Classrooms are newly set up in 2019. The number of Chinese learners around the world has climbed to 150 million, and the "circle of friends" of international Chinese language education is expanding considerably.

3. Construction and Cultivation of Talent Teams

By the end of 2019, the Confucius Institute Headquarters had sent 3,633 teachers to 155 countries (regions), including 3,006 teachers to 416 Confucius Institutes and 66 Confucius Classrooms in 152 countries (regions), and 627 teachers to foreign universities, primary and secondary schools (non-Confucius Institutes).

In 2019, the Confucius Institute Headquarters have supported 17 foreign universities in 12 countries to establish Chinese Language Education major, and have trained a total of 6,930 teachers for 7 South Asian countries, including 74 South Asian teachers who came to China to train. It has also employed 219 local teachers from 43 countries. 35 Confucius Institutes in 16 countries have employed 36 core Confucius Institute teachers.

In 2019, 6,520 postgraduates were enrolled in 148 institutions with TCSOL Master's degree authorization. The 19 institutions with Doctor of Education degree authorization have recruited 59 doctoral students of TCSOL. 1,269 students in Chinese Language Education major have been cultivated in total.

Over 14,000 people applied to participate in the volunteer program in 2019, and 6,289 volunteer teachers were selected and sent to 140 countries and regions to teach Chinese.

4. Academic Exchanges

In January 2019, *Chinese Teaching in the World* hosted the "Seminar on Characteristics and Construction of Knowledge System of Chinese Language International Education"; in May, "The 2nd Symposium on International Chinese Language Teacher Training and Development and Digitalized Chinese Language Teaching" was held in Beijing Foreign Studies University; in June, Beijing Language and Culture University Press hosted the "Symposium on Case-based TCSOL Pedagogy and Teaching Models", and the editorial board of *Chinese Teaching in the World* and Qingdao University held the "Symposium on International Chinese Education in the New Era"; in July, the conference "Acquisition of Chinese: Bilingualism and Multilingualism" supported by "Confucius China Studies Program" was held in the University of Cambridge; in August, the International Society for Chinese Language Teaching hosted the "Advanced Workshop on International Chinese Language Education Teaching and Research"; in September, *Language Teaching and Linguistic Studies* hosted the "Forum on Frontiers of Language Teaching and Research and the 40th Anniversary Celebration of *Language Teaching and Linguistic Studies*"; in October, the International Conference on Chinese as a Second Language (ICCSL-16) and the 4th International Conference on Teaching Chinese (ICTC-4) was co-hosted by the Research Institute of International Chinese Language Education of Beijing Language and Culture University and other institutions; in November, the National Education Steering Committee for MTCSOL Graduate Students organized "The 1st High-Level National Forum on TCSOL Doctoral Talents Cultivation".

In December 2019, the International Chinese Language Education Conference was held in Changsha with the theme of "Innovation and Development of International Chinese Language Education in the New Era". Over 1,000 representatives of Confucius Institutes and Chinese language education institutions from more than 160 countries and regions attended the conference.

5. Overseas Cooperation

As of November 2019, a total of 69 countries and regions in the world have incorporated Chinese language teaching into their national education systems by issuing laws, decrees, syllabuses and curricula, etc., such as South Africa, Mauritius, Tanzania, Cameroon, Zambia and other African countries; Thailand, Malaysia and other Southeast Asian countries have formed a complete Chinese teaching system from pre-school education, compulsory education, vocational education to higher education through promulgating policies and regulations; the United States, Canada, Japan, South Korea, Australia, Russia and other countries have successively listed Chinese as one of the foreign language subjects in the university entrance examination.

In 2019, the Confucius Institute Headquarters signed a cooperation agreement with Briusov National University of Languages and Social Sciences of Erevan in Armenia (in June) and the University of Alvador in France (in July) on supporting the Chinese language education programs (Teaching Chinese as a Foreign Language); built the Chinese Language Center with North Korea's Pyongyang University of Foreign Studies (in September); signed a cooperation agreement with Portugal (in April) and the United Arab Emirates (in July) to incorporate Chinese language into their national primary and secondary education systems; assisted Belgium in writing Chinese language syllabus (in November); the International Society for Chinese Language Teaching supported South Africa to formally register and set up the Chinese Language Teachers Association (in February), and approved the membership of the American "Chinese as a Second Language Research Association" (in April).

III. Prospect

At the 2019 International Chinese Education Conference, Vice Premier of the State Council Sun Chunlan at that time put forward three principles for the development of international Chinese language education: first, focus on the language, actively integrate into the local area, incorporate special courses in language teaching to meet the needs of bilateral cooperation, and actively promote "Chinese + vocational skills" programs; second, revise and popularize evaluation standards, improve teaching quality, and develop educational syllabuses and localized textbooks according to local conditions; third, follow the international practice in language dissemination, adhere to market-oriented operations, and support Chinese and foreign universities, enterprises as well as social organizations to establish international non-governmental foundations, and establish extensive contacts with educational, cultural, media, think tanks and other institutions in various countries in order to promote the diversification of school-running entities.

Chen Baosheng, Minister of Education at that time also proposed six new measures to support the sustainable and high-quality development of international Chinese language education:

(1) Improve the international Chinese education system for undergraduates, masters and doctors, and support Chinese universities to independently set up professional doctorate degree and greatly increase the number of professional doctorates.

(2) Support Chinese universities to establish international Chinese language teacher colleges, and cooperate with foreign universities to establish Chinese language teacher colleges, which not only recruit students for degree programs, but also conduct various professional trainings.

(3) Formulate policies to improve the welfare of Chinese teachers and volunteers sent abroad, and support Confucius Institutes in various countries to select and hire more local Chinese language teachers.

(4) Support Chinese and foreign experts to jointly develop high-quality textbooks

and compile Chinese textbooks with both global generality and local adaptability. Meanwhile, strengthen the construction of digital resources, upgrade Confucius Institute Online for a better global Chinese learning platform.

(5) Improve the international Chinese language education standards, strengthen the evaluation and monitoring of teaching quality, and formulate policies that take the HSK score as an important benchmark for learners from all over the world to study in China.

(6) Continue supporting and encouraging the participation of various school enterprises, social organizations, and individuals in China as well as other countries, especially Chinese and foreign universities, to take more part in the construction of Confucius Institutes and international Chinese language education through various means, such as jointly establishing foundations, so as to better play their roles as the main players in international Chinese language education.

Looking to the future, international Chinese language education has a long way to go. With the changing international environment, the awareness of a community with a shared future for mankind will continue strengthening, and the "Belt and Road" Initiative will constantly expand its construction. In light of both challenges and opportunities, it is necessary to further assess the situation, deepen reforms, and keep pace with the times in a spirit of pioneering and innovative. Thus, we are able to advance the steady and long-term development of international Chinese language education through continuous innovation.

In the aspects of discipline construction and talent development, efforts can be made to strengthen the construction of the "five systems":

(1) We need to build an integrated Chinese language teacher education system from undergraduates, masters to doctors. At the same time, we will explore a new educational system with different focuses throughout the integrated process of cultivation, providing outstanding students with opportunities for further studies.

(2) We need to construct a Chinese language teacher education system with differentiated training and diversified development: diversified Chinese language teachers are cultivated for overseas or domestic universities and colleges, international schools;

education administrators and educational resource developers are trained for Confucius Institutes and Chinese language programs both at home and abroad; teacher education experts are cultivated for the discipline and major of international Chinese language education.

(3) We need to build a Chinese language teacher education system that integrates "degree education" and "teacher training".

(4) We need to build a Chinese language teacher education system opening up to international students and cultivate high-quality Chinese language teachers and education administrators for overseas Chinese teaching institutions.

(5) We need to formulate evaluation standards and systems for Chinese language teachers. In the aspect of Chinese language teacher education, it is necessary not only to train teachers, but also to establish effective evaluation standards.

(Liu Li, Beijing Language and Culture University)

Report on International Chinese Language Education Research

International Chinese language education is a very distinctive field of education and teaching. Each step of its development is closely connected with the needs of cultural and people-to-people exchanges as well as mutual learning between Chinese and foreign civilizations, and also shows the characteristics of discipline construction. From the perspective of academic research, this distinctive field will inevitably present characteristics not possessed by general disciplines in terms of internal and external environment, the targeted clients and knowledge system, and demonstrate a distinctive contemporary relevance. Over the years, international Chinese language education has been flourishing in discipline construction, academic research and cause development, but there is an urgency to address some potential problems affecting its sustainable development.

I. Topics of Concern in Recent Years

After summarizing the research of international Chinese language education in recent years, we can find the basic topics focus on the following aspects, some of which have formed a clear consensus, while others are still controversial.

1. The Relationship Between the Discipline and the Cause

International Chinese language education is a cause, a discipline, and a profession. Therefore, the relationship between the discipline and the cause has been a fundamental issue we have to face in its development process. In contrast, "TCFL" for international students, which emerged from the needs of the cause, has made outstanding achievements in its discipline construction. Since Chinese language teaching at that time was mainly engaged in teaching Chinese as a foreign language within China, the relationship between the discipline and the cause was not prominent. At the beginning of this century when Chinese language teaching developed to the stage of "international Chinese language education", overseas Chinese language education has made great achievements unprecedentedly as a cause. However, the construction of relevant disciplines has not started simultaneously, and the relationship between the discipline and the cause, especially the problem of playing down the importance of the discipline, has come to the fore. In recent years, the existence and development of the discipline has been under discussion as a fundamental issue among the academia, and there has been a growing call for equal emphasis on "discipline" research and "cause" development.

2. The Nature and Orientation of the Discipline

There has always been controversy over whether the discipline of international Chinese language education belongs to that of Chinese Language and Literature, or to that of Pedagogy, or it is an emerging interdisciplinary discipline that is taking shape. At present, the undergraduate program of TCSOL is listed under the first-level discipline of "Chinese Language and Literature" in the category of "Literature", and TCSOL Master's degree is under the first-level discipline of "Pedagogy", which has led to much discussion. The unclear positioning in academic disciplines has a direct influence on the setting of programs, curriculum system, training objectives, etc. The current situation is that the linguistic field puts much emphasis on its disciplinary affiliation, while the education field seems to be less concerned with that. Its disciplinary teaching content is mostly based on language and linguistics as well as relevant disciplines, while pedagogy-related content is only offered as a few auxiliary courses. It follows that it should be more reasonable to position international Chinese language education in favor of linguistics.

3. The Basic Functions of International Chinese Language Education

Language is an important carrier of culture, and the function of language teaching is directly related to both language and culture. The academic circles have different views on whether the basic function of international Chinese language education is based on language education or cultural promotion. Over the years, the major understanding is to advocate a return to the essence of language education, that is to say, taking the teaching of Chinese language and characters as the basis and realizing other functions in language teaching through special strategies. At this moment, new issues are posed for international Chinese language education: how to reflect Chinese cultural characteristics through international Chinese language education, and further, how to make new contributions to building a community with a shared future for mankind.

4. The Disciplinary Knowledge System

If international Chinese language education is viewed as an independent discipline or an emerging interdisciplinary field, the primary task is to construct a disciplinary knowledge system, because it is the key factor in determining the scientific level of international Chinese language education. The academia has already recognized that the disciplinary system of international Chinese language education should include at least three parts: the first is the basic theories supporting the discipline, which refer to the basic disciplines supporting the development of international Chinese language education, such as linguistics, pedagogy, and psychology; the second is the theoretical system underlying the discipline, which refers to the basic theories of the international Chinese language education itself, such as the knowledge of Chinese linguistics, social and cultural knowledge for international Chinese language education, second language acquisition and teaching theory of Chinese as a second language as well as the basic research methods of related disciplines; the third is the applied research of discipline construction, which refers to applying discipline theories to the specialized research on overall design, educational management, teacher training, teaching materials development, classroom teaching, testing and assessment, resource construction, etc., as well as the use and research of educational technology and skills, and the applied research itself also has its own underlying theories. How to build a disciplinary system for international Chinese language education that meets the needs of discipline construction and development as well as highlights the discipline's own characteristics and rules in the new era is a major issue in discipline construction.

5. Teachers, Textbooks and Teaching Methods

The "three T's" (teachers, textbooks, and teaching methods) have been widely discussed in international Chinese language education. The problems of the "three T's" have become more complex as the implementation of international Chinese language education is mainly conducted in foreign countries, and the learner groups are getting more diversified, with more young learners. In particular, localization, country-specific, language-specific and nationality-specific issues are all reflected in every aspect of the three T's. Thus, studies on teacher resources and training, on the research and compilation of differentiated textbooks, and on accommodating teaching strategies in light of the textbooks and students have drawn extensive attention.

6. Overseas Chinese Language Education

Apart from non-Chinese learners, the target learners of international Chinese language education also include overseas Chinese naturalized in foreign countries or Chinese citizens and their children residing abroad for a long time. Therefore, overseas Chinese language education for Chinese ethnic groups is an important and unique component of international Chinese language education. Because of the diversity and complexity of language and culture, overseas Chinese language education for Chinese ethnic groups is distinct and rich in its depth. The knowledge system has significant differences as to the teaching of Chinese as a second/foreign language despite much in common in the general sense, so the specialized research is conducted on the curriculum and course design, textbook development, classroom teaching, testing and assessment, teacher training, and learning characteristics, and these have become heated topics in recent years.

7. Construction and Development of Confucius Institutes

Confucius Institutes had been under construction for 15 years and have entered a phase of developing in depth from expanding in scope. Regarding the construction of Confucius Institutes, the national policy, management system, operation mechanism, development concept, construction ecology and faculty, curriculum design, teaching resources and teaching mode all need to be further studied in the new global situation.

8. Development of Online Teaching and Construction of the Platform and Resources

With the development of information technology, the ecosystem of international Chinese language education has undergone fundamental changes, and the "cloud teaching" model in the mobile Internet era is gradually taking shape. In recent years, international Chinese language education has strengthened the construction of various educational and teaching platforms as well as resource information bases, and conducted research projects based on relevant resource bases. These platforms and resource bases include webcasting platforms, MOOC, online courses and corpora, teaching material library, textbook database, banks of teaching cases, teaching courseware, supplementary teaching materials, and collections of treatises. Among them, relatively developed are those of linguistic studies and second language acquisition studies which are based on corpus and textbook database.

II. Pressing Issues

Considering the historic mission and current situation of international Chinese education, there are pressing problems in both the cause development and the discipline construction. From the perspective of its discipline construction and development, I'd like to concisely illustrate several outstanding aspects.

1. Indistinct Relationship Between International Chinese Language Education as the Cause and TCSOL as the Discipline

Because of its dual nature and mission, it is normal for the two to have overlap fields. However, if discipline construction is taken or obscured as only a cause, then its development will probably be neglected and restricted, especially in the overall design, the allocation of resources, the construction of human resources, the basic theory research, and academic achievements in application.

2. Unclear Understanding of Disciplinary Positioning and Dimensions

This is a long-standing issue—not clearly defining the positioning of TCSOL and its dimensions has always been controversial in both TCFL phase and in the current stage of TCSOL/international Chinese language education. Someone considers TCSOL as a sub-discipline of linguistics (part of applied linguistics), or a sub-discipline of pedagogy, or an interdiscipline between linguistics and pedagogy, or an independent emerging interdiscipline, whereas someone considers it to be closely related to communication as its main task is to promote the spread of Chinese culture. Diversified argument foundations lead to different views in the academia, so the discipline develops without a clear direction and often swings to and fro.

3. Incomplete Disciplinary Knowledge System

Owing to the lack of clarity in the discipline's positioning, the academia has not reached a consensus on what constitutes the disciplinary knowledge system of TCSOL. It is broadly clear that the basic theories underpinning the discipline include those from linguistics, pedagogy, and psychology, but the relationship between linguistics and pedagogy in the system of basic knowledge is not clear. At present, the pedagogy field does not pay close attention to the research and development of TCSOL, which is mainly driven by linguistics field; while, as for the pedagogical principles in TCSOL, the linguists do not show much interest. In addition to these basic disciplines, the basic theoretical system of TCSOL and the applied research within it are not adequately studied either.

4. Insufficient Overall Planning and Top-Level Design

Since the beginning of the new century, compared with the discipline construction phase of teaching Chinese as a foreign language, the overall design of the international Chinese language education at discipline level is basically in a spontaneous development state in many aspects, and the strategic top-level design of the discipline is not in shape yet. Especially in the new period, considering the development of Confucius Institutes and overseas Chinese language teaching, the increasing popularity and the low age of the learners, the increase of differentiated Chinese teaching courses, and the promotion of preparatory programs, we need to redesign long-term plans for every aspect and every link from the holistic view and top level. There is a fact need to be specially noted that the lack of overall and top-level design will directly lead to the absence of guidance from relevant academic societies, and that will hold up the disciplinary development of international Chinese language education. Thus, the academia and administrators need to rethink and redefine the role of academic societies and associations.

5. Research of Fundamental Theories Lacking Depth

As a discipline with a relatively short history and greatly different mentalities of the stakeholders, research of fundamental theories of international Chinese language education needs to be carried out comprehensively and deeply. At present, domestic and overseas situations change rapidly. Against that background, we can enhance the scientific, complete, predictable and adaptable discipline construction only by doing solid theoretical research, applied research, research on teaching practice and other basic research. In particular, the basic theoretical construction of Confucius Institutes and Confucius Classrooms is to be conducted. Thus, there is an urgent need to conduct systematic study in these aspects for the sustainable development of international Chinese language education.

6. Unfavorable Innovation Mechanism for Cultivating Multi-Tiered and High-Level Talents

Due to the dual nature of international Chinese language education as mentioned before, it is essential to cultivate not only research-oriented and teaching talents for the discipline, or the managerial talents in light of the cause development, but also the versatile talents with both characteristics. Now, the innovation mechanism of talents training at all levels is not in place yet. And it is not uncommon to see belated efforts in cultivating the personnel for urgent needs. Moreover, personnel cultivation is less targeted or not well planned. In cultivating high-level talents, we now put much emphasis on Master's degree and Doctor's degree programs without paying enough attention to other aspects of personnel cultivation. In particular, it is necessary to make top-level design and overall planning on the national level for the training and human resources building of overseas teachers and managerial personnel abroad.

(Shi Chunhong, Beijing Language and Culture University)

II Itemized Reports

Report on the Development of International Chinese Language Teachers

After the founding of the People's Republic of China, TCFL was initiated as the "Special Chinese Language Course for Exchange Students in Eastern Europe", which was launched in Tsinghua University in July of 1950 and Chinese language teaching started in early 1951, with 33 international students and 6 Chinese teachers. In 1961, the Department of Higher Education selected Chinese language teachers and sent them abroad (1961-1964), which was the beginning for TCFL teachers training. In the summer of 1965, Beijing Language Institute designed the first teacher training course for Chinese language teachers of international students. In 1978, a 4-year (Bachelor's) degree program "Modern Chinese Language" was set in Beijing Language Institute, which specifically trained TCFL teachers. Following that, in the 1980s and 1990s, Bachelor's degree, Master's degree, and Doctor's degree in TCSOL were established in succession, specifically to train the teachers related to teaching Chinese as a second language.

I. Talents Cultivation

Teacher training for TCFL is a long-term process that involves continuous professional learning in classroom, self-study outside classroom, participation in teaching practice, step-by-step correction of mistakes, establishment of professional attitude and awareness, and eventually become a mature and experienced Chinese language teacher.

In order to meet the increasing demand for international Chinese language teachers from overseas, China has made great efforts to promote the development of TCSOL and constantly improve the training system for international Chinese language teachers. So far, apart from TCSOL undergraduate program, talents training of TCSOL teachers mainly involves two levels: Master's degree and Doctor's degree and cover four types: academic MA students, academic doctoral students, professional MA students, and professional doctoral students. According to statistics, in 2019, there were more than 100 colleges and universities in China engaged in the teacher training related to international Chinese language education, distributed in 29 provinces, autonomous regions, and municipalities except for Qinghai Province and Tibet Autonomous Region (Hong Kong, Macao and Taiwan were not included in this statistics).

1. Academic MA Students

Since the 1990s, MA degree related to TCSOL has been established, marking the beginning of high-level talents cultivation in TCSOL field. MA degree programs require 3-year full-time learning.

In 2019, 82 universities and colleges nationwide enrolled MA students in Linguistics and Applied Linguistics (TCSOL as an orientation), but since 2006, when professional Master's degree programs in TCSOL began, more students have been recruited on professional Master's degree programs, instead of academic MA programs. At present, the number of academic MA students is much smaller than that of professional MA students.

2. Academic Doctoral Students

In 1997, the State Council Academic Degrees Committee approved the establishment of "Linguistics and Applied Linguistics" (No. 050102) as an authorized doctoral program, and started recruiting students. In 2015, Beijing Language and Culture University autonomously established "TCSOL" Doctor's degree program as a secondary discipline, which is the first Doctor's degree titled TCSOL (i.e., TCFL) in China. This is a 3-to-4-year PhD program.

In 2019, 79 students for PhD degree in TCSOL and its relevant fields were recruited in 59 universities and institutions.

3. Professional MA Students

In order to meet the growing demand for Chinese language teachers around the world, the professional Master's degree program in international Chinese language teaching (later entitled MTCSOL) began enrollment in 2006. In 2007, the program was officially listed in the MA catalog, and the official enrollment began in colleges and universities nationwide from 2008. Professional Master's degree in TCSOL is usually a 2-to-3-year program. At the very beginning, colleges and universities opt for two-year full-time degree programs, but the recent years witnessed a gradual increasing number of colleges and universities opting for three-year programs. As of 2018, there are 148 colleges and universities offering professional Master's degree program in TCSOL nationwide, cultivating around 48,000 students over the past decade.

In 2019, 148 colleges and universities in China enrolled 6,520 professional Master students, including 5,209 Chinese and 1,311 international students. As of 2019, statistics showed that about 55,000 professional Master students in TCSOL have been cultivated, with about 43,000 Chinese and 12,000 international students.

With the largest number of Chinese language teachers in China's TCSOL teacher training system, MTCSOL also ranks the top in supplying Chinese language teachers abroad now. Therefore, this type of talents training is a paramount and prominent undertaking. Every year, a number of professional forums nationwide are held dedicated to discussing the issues concerning MTCSOL. According to the survey, in addition to the mandatory courses "Overview of Chinese Acquisition as a Second Language", "Introduction to the Acquisition of Chinese as a Second Language", "An Introduction to Chinese Culture", "Intercultural Communication & Interactions", "Class Organization & Management" and other optional courses in culture, language education and pedagogy, the features of the curriculum of MTCSOL teacher education highlight teaching practice courses and the required one-year overseas teaching internship implemented by some universities.

4. Professional Doctoral Students

In 2018, in order to improve the quality of international Chinese language education talents training and to cultivate high-level versatile talents in Chinese language education both at home and abroad as well as the international communication of Chinese culture, the Ministry of Education approved 12 colleges and universities to pilot the enrollment of professional doctoral students of TCSOL. In the same year, 7 Chinese universities recruited 22 students for professional doctoral degree in TCSOL, which is usually 4-to-6-year in length, for learners in-service.

According to statistics, 19 colleges and universities nationwide enrolled 59 professional doctoral students of TCSOL in 2019. By the end of 2019, there were 81 doctoral students of TCSOL in 19 colleges and universities.

In 2019, enrollment on Master's degree and Doctor's degree programs of the four types above reached over 7,000 in 148 colleges and universities nationwide.

In conclusion, the current TCSOL teacher education shows the following characteristics: first, with the integration of the cultivation system for undergraduates, MA students (academic and professional), and doctoral students (academic and professional) in related majors, the talents cultivation system is well-developed, which provides a strong guarantee for meeting the demand for international Chinese language education as well as alleviating the shortage of teachers, and reserves talents pool for the development of TCSOL; second, the cultivation of MTCSOL is an important guarantee for the supply of practical teaching talents in international Chinese language education and is one of its core tasks for sustainable development. After years of efforts and development, the shortage of overseas Chinese language teachers has been greatly alleviated.

In 2019, China also supported 17 universities in 12 countries to establish Chinese Language Teacher Education program to specialize in the training of local Chinese language teachers.

II. Teacher Training

In order to meet the needs of improving the competence of Chinese language teachers abroad, China has provided various training programs for overseas local Chinese language teachers and the teachers sent by China to all over the world.

1. Training of Chinese Language Teachers

(1) Pre-service training for Chinese sponsored teachers

According to statistics, a total of 925 new sponsored Chinese language teachers were trained and sent to teach in 155 countries.

(2) Training of overseas teachers in China

According to statistics, 953 overseas Chinese language teachers from 56 countries were trained in 2019.

(3) Chinese experts going abroad to train local teachers

Statistics show that China sent Chinese expert teams to 13 countries to train 783 local Chinese language teachers in 2019.

2. Training of Volunteer Chinese Teachers

(1) Pre-service training for volunteer Chinese teachers

Statistics indicate that nearly 4,700 new volunteer Chinese language teachers were trained and sent to 140 countries in 2019.

(2) On-the-job training for volunteer Chinese teachers

According to statistics, a total of 17 countries carried out on-the-job training for volunteer Chinese teachers, with more than 3,700 teachers trained in 2019.

In summary, in 2019, China trained 1,736 overseas local teachers, 925 new sponsored teachers, and more than 8,400 volunteer Chinese teachers (including pre-service and on-the-job training). More than 11,000 teachers of various types have been trained for international Chinese language education through the whole year of 2019.

III. Overseas Teachers

In 2019, in response to the needs of Chinese language teachers overseas, China sent 9,922 Chinese language teachers (including sponsored Chinese teachers and volunteer Chinese teachers) to 155 countries after selection and training. Among them, 6,289 volunteer Chinese teachers were sent to 140 countries (and regions) to teach Chinese language, and 3,633 sponsored teachers were sent to universities, primary and secondary schools in 155 countries. Among the sponsored teachers, 3,006 were sent to 416 Confucius Institutes and 66 Confucius Classrooms in 152 countries, and 627 were sent to universities, primary and secondary schools that were not affiliated with Confucius Institutes. As for volunteer Chinese teachers, 3,031 of them worked in Confucius Institutes (Classrooms), and 3,258 worked in local universities, primary and secondary schools that were not affiliated with Confucius Institutes (Classrooms).

219 local Chinese language teachers were employed in 43 countries along the route of "Belt and Road" in 2019.

Judging from the demand for Chinese language teachers from overseas, and the supply of sponsored teachers and volunteer Chinese teachers provided by China, as well as the pipeline of Master students of TCSOL in China, a balance has been basically achieved in 2019 between the demand and the supply.

(Zhu Ruiping, Liu Xu, Beijing Normal University)

Report on the Development of International Chinese Language Education Textbooks

I. Construction History of Textbooks

Modern Chinese Reader (Deng, 1958) was the first textbook for Chinese as a foreign language published after the founding of the People's Republic of China in 1949, and *Chinese Textbook* was published in Bulgaria during the same time (Zhu & Zhang, 1954).

Since the reform and opening up in 1978, textbook construction has been in progress with the development of international Chinese language education. After established in 1987, Hanban has vigorously promoted the research and development of Chinese textbooks. By the end of 2013, the Confucius Institute Headquarters have developed about 3,000 Chinese language textbooks, including the textbooks for universities, primary and secondary schools, self-study textbooks and handbooks, reading materials, reference books, examination materials, teaching standards and outlines, etc., which comprise the basic framework of Chinese language textbooks. By 2017, more than 30 million textbooks have been distributed to 170 countries. Moreover, the Confucius Institute Digital Library has provided digital resources of language, culture, humanities and social sciences.

Since the 21st century, the research and development of international Chinese language textbooks have shown new characteristics and trends: (1) The publication scale has surged phenomenally: altogether 1,373 volumes/types (accounting for 13.6%) of textbooks were published before 2000, while 8,735 volumes/types (86.4%) were published in the first 20 years of this century. (2) The textbooks were published in more languages. They have 16 languages versions in the last century, while more than 40 language versions were added in the first 20 years of this century. (3) The proportion of children's textbooks has increased sharply: in the last century, there were 242 volumes/types, accounting for 17.63% of the total number of textbooks; while the first 20 years of this century has produced 2,883 volumes/types of children's textbooks, accounting for 33.01% in total. (4) Specialized textbooks were less than 1% in the last century, while over 5% textbooks are for special purposes in the first 20 years of this century. By the end of 2018, the Global Chinese Teaching Material E-library of the Base for International Chinese Teaching Materials Development and Teacher Training has collected more than 17,800 volumes/types of international Chinese language textbooks in use, which were published in 40 countries and in 56 languages. The global development trends of Chinese language textbooks are as follows: first, the focus transfers from centering on language elements to integrating language, communication and culture; second, teaching methods are diversified; third, communication skills are more specified.

II. Current Situation at Home

The statistics of textbooks from 22 publishers by the end of 2019 are as follows: 667 total volumes/types were published in 16 languages (including Chinese, English, Korean, French, Russian, German, Arabic, Spanish, Indonesian, Thai, Mongolian, Romanian, Czech, Dutch, Polish, Hausa, bilingual or multilingual).

1. Textbooks and Reading Materials

There are 140 volumes/types of classroom textbooks published in China, including 131 volumes/types of general textbooks and 9 volumes/types of specialized textbooks to meet the needs of Chinese language teaching in the new era. For instance, *Intensive Chinese for Pre-University Students* (6 volumes) published by Beijing Language and Culture University Press (BLCUP) and *Learning in China* (4 volumes) published by Foreign Language Teaching and Research Press (FLTRP) closely follow the *Syllabus of the Final Exam for Pre-University International Students in China with Chinese Government Scholarships* to cater for the international students studying for academic degrees in China. There are some textbooks tailored for the students who want to learn specialized Chinese language and to study for academic degrees, such as *A Series of Specialized Chinese Textbooks for Foreigner Studying in China—Chinese for Science and Technology: Physics* published by Beijing Language and Culture University Press, *Thesis Reading and Writing for International Students* published by Huazhong University of Science and Technology Press and *Thesis Writing* published by Jinan University Press. *Peking University MOOCs Textbook: Chinese Characters* published by the Commercial Press is compiled to support "Peking University MOOCs—Chinese Characters", and is synchronized with the online course.

Classroom textbooks pay more attention to the needs of learners of different ages. In 2019, 93 volumes/types of textbooks for adult students, 29 for secondary schools and 18 for primary schools were developed. Among them, adult textbooks include *Expressway to Chinese* published by BLCUP, *Boya Chinese* by Peking University Press (PUP), *Mastering Chinese* by People's Education Press, and *Contemporary Chinese (Mongolian/Polish/Czech Edition)* by Sinolingua Press, etc. Textbooks for secondary schools include *Hey Chinese!* and *Everyday Chinese—Chinese Course Book for Middle Schools in Thailand,* both were published by BLCUP; textbooks for primary schools include *I Love Chinese—Chinese Textbook for Thai Primary School* by FLTRP, and *Lively Chinese* by Sinolingua Press, etc.

Six textbooks and handbooks for self-study have been published since there is no much demand for self-study books due to the abundant resources of Chinese language learning in China.

There are 454 volumes/types of reading materials, accounting for 68.1% of the overall number of Chinese language textbooks published in China, 415 of which are children's books, accounting for 91.4% of reading materials in China. The contents cover a wide range, including humanities, national conditions of China, daily/campus life, science, etc., most of which are series of graded readings.

2. Reference Books and Supplementary Teaching Materials

There are 7 volumes/types of reference books, such as *Advanced Chinese-English Dictionary of Chinese Usage (Illustrated)* published by Sinolingua and *Concise Chinese Dictionary* (in two versions) published by FLTRP. The latter is an elementary Chinese-French and Chinese-German bilingual dictionary. The Chinese words in it are those of high-frequency in the *HSK Test Syllabus* and *Lexicon of Common Words in Contemporary Chinese,* and the dictionary is illustrated.

There are 36 volumes/types of test preparation books. Most of them are HSK preparation textbooks, such as *Frequency-based HSK Vocabulary* and *Chinese Character Book for HSK.* There are also mock tests for IBDP Chinese language tests and IGCSE/IBDP, etc.

There are 24 volumes/types of textbooks for teacher development. For instance, *TCSOL Pedagogy* published by Higher Education Press (HEP) introduces teaching methods, teaching links, methods and skills. *The Teaching of International Chinese Starts from Here: Cases and Analyses of the Teaching of International Chinese in Primary and Secondary Schools* published by PUP collects 60 real teaching cases from 13 countries.

III. Current Situation Abroad

By the end of 2019, there had been 598 volumes/types of textbooks in 10 languages in 12 countries where Chinese language education developed relatively well with their own features.

1. Textbooks and Reading Materials

There are 246 volumes/types of classroom textbooks abroad, including 237 general Chinese textbooks, 9 specialized Chinese books (3 for tourism, 2 for business, 1 for judiciary, i.e., *Chinese Judicial Interpretation Theory and Cases* in Korea, 1 for aviation, i.e., *Practical Chinese for Aviation* in Korea, 1 for medical Chinese and 1 for marketing). Textbooks tailored to different age groups include 151 volumes/types for college students and adults, 24 for secondary school students, 68 for primary school students, and 3 for preschoolers. Adult textbooks include *New Horizon Chinese* in Japan, *Eyes on China: An Intermediate-Advanced Reader of Modern Chinese* in English-speaking area, and *Ternyata Bahasa Mandarin Mudah* in Indonesia. Textbooks for secondary school students include *Viaje a China* in Spain and *Step up with Chinese* in Singapore. For primary school students, there are textbooks such as *China Study Grades 1-6* in Egypt, *Chinois: le guide de conversation des enfants* in France, and *Happy Learning Chinese* in Thailand.

There are 144 volumes/types of textbooks and handbooks for self-study abroad, far more than those published in China, mainly covering speaking, listening, vocabulary (including flash cards), Chinese characters and grammar, etc., such as *Next Steps in Mandarin Chinese with Paul Noble for Intermediate Learners* published by HarperCollins Publishers LLC and *Chinesische Handelskorrespondenz* in Germany.

There are 113 volumes/types of reading materials, 96 of which are children's reading materials, mostly literary stories, including paper books, e-books and audio recorded books. For instance, *World Chinese Graded Readers* of Cengage in Singapore is graded into 10 levels, covering stories, popular science, and Chinese culture; 50 volumes/types among the series came out, sold mainly in the United States, Indonesia, and the Philippines.

2. Reference Books and Supplementary Teaching Materials

There are 17 volumes/types of reference books mainly for adults. Most of them are dictionaries and grammar books, and books for learning Chinese characters are also included. Among these reference books, 2 are picture dictionaries for children.

There are 73 volumes/types of test preparation books, and the contents are mostly vocabulary exercises and practice/mock tests. Those books are mainly for HSK, including *Easy Writing HSK 3 Full Chinese Simplified Characters Vocabulary* and *Sailing Through New HSK 1*. There are also books for YCT, such as *Dream Chinese YCT,* and also for other tests, such as *AP Chinese Vocabulary Book Version*

2019, Intermediate Examination Level 3 Writing Problem Thorough Measures 1,000 Questions, and *IB Chinese B (HL) Chinese Intensive Revision.* These test coaching materials overlap certain secondary school textbooks, such as *Cambridge IGCSE® Chinese as a Second Language* series published by Cambridge University Press, which is based on the IGCSE Chinese as a Second Language Syllabus.

There are also 5 volumes/types of textbooks for teacher training, some of which are teaching guides, such as *Primary Chinese Teaching Toolkit;* others are studies on teaching and learners, such as *Teaching Chinese as a Second Language: The Way of the Learner.*

IV. Features of Textbook Construction

1. The proportion of reading materials and teacher training textbooks published in China is higher than those published overseas, while classroom textbooks, self-study books and handbooks, reference books, and test preparation books of overseas publications account for a higher proportion than those published in China. The two complement each other.

2. Children's textbooks account for 33.4% of classroom textbooks and children's reading materials for 91.1% of overall reading materials. The proportion of children's textbooks published overseas is significantly higher than that in China, as Chinese language has been introduced into the national education systems of over 60 countries and there are many children learners overseas.

3. Textbooks for "Chinese + vocational skills" program have increased. In line with the needs of the "Belt and Road" Initiative, future will witness much growth in the textbooks for "Chinese + vocational skills". Those books include *Chinese for Working Professionals—A Textbook for Intermediate-High to Advanced Learners* published by Routledge in Britain, *Go to China, Learn Technology* (including the content in railway, logistics, and e-commerce) used in the Confucius Institute at Khon Kaen University in Thailand, *Policing Chinese* by FLTRP of Beijing, China and *Chinese for Cabin Crews*

by New Sharing Publisher of Taiwan, China. Some Confucius Institutes/Classrooms in Africa have compiled textbooks (unpublished) on their own, such as *Teaching Materials for Tourist Guides* by the Confucius Institute at University of Namibia, *Chinese for Seychelles Aviation* and *Chinese for Seychelles Tourism* by the Confucius Institute at University of Seychelles and *Nursing Chinese* by the Confucius Institute at University of Sierra Leone. Open University of China Press has developed *Industrial Chinese* series, and *Welding Technology* among the series has been on trial in Zambia.

4. The number of textbooks in the areas where textbooks used to be scarce has increased. For example, in the Arabic language area, there are *China Study Grades 1-6* (bilingual version in Chinese and Arabic) co-published by Bayt Alhekma Cultural Investment Company in Egypt and East China Normal University Press (ECNUP) in China, as well as the secondary school textbook *Across the Silk Road* (unpublished) promoted by the Ministry of Education of the UAE. In Africa, Confucius Institutes/Classrooms developed textbooks on their own (see the previous section), such as *Life in Literature* published in Mozambique. A point-reading textbook, *The Story of Xiao Li*, is published in 8 languages by International Express Chinese Education Press of Hong Kong, China and widely used in Kazakhstan international schools.

5. Textbooks for teacher training are prioritized, the contents of which are mainly pedagogy, teaching cases, and teaching skills, such as *Teaching with Ms. Gan* and *50 Games for the International Chinese Classroom.* In order to adapt to the discipline construction and address the problem of shortage of qualified teachers, the publishers, such as BLCUP, PUP, are conducting several series of textbooks projects.

6. Research on textbooks is imbalanced. 113 papers on international Chinese textbooks are retrieved from CNKI by keywords, including 9 on the publication information of textbooks, 6 and 98 respectively on textbooks published before and after the founding of the People's Republic of China. Among the 98 papers, most study textbooks used in Chinese universities; only 6 papers study textbooks which are oriented to primary and secondary school students, 3 papers on reading materials, 11 papers on overseas textbooks and the localization of textbooks abroad, and 8 papers on specialized

Chinese, which account for a relatively low proportion.

7. The direction for future development is clearer. In the future, we should focus on textbook localization, developing age-appropriate textbooks as well as the specialized textbooks (for profession and occupation) and pay attention to the construction of online educational resources so as to meet the global demand for Chinese language education. Meanwhile, we should timely make the most use of the research results of second language teaching and acquisition as well as of the textbooks around the world in teaching practice and pay attention to the theoretical construction and practical effects of teaching materials.

(Zhou Xiaobing, Beijing Language and Culture University; Wang Xi, East China Normal University)

Report on the Development of Chinese Proficiency Tests

The year of 2019 marks a new start for international Chinese language education, an important historical juncture, and a new beginning for the development of Chinese proficiency tests. It has been 35 years since the establishment of HSK in 1984, and 15 years since the first Confucius Institute was set up in the world in 2004. During this period, HSK as well as other Chinese tests have developed vigorously to meet the demand. It is a new start for HSK to change from "*hanyu*" to "*zhongwen*" and from "exam" to "test". It not only shows a change of words, but also demonstrates the new look and profound concept of international Chinese language education in the new era: returning to the nature of equal importance on both "spoken language" and "written characters" and focusing more on learning processes than on results in developing systematic tests. In 2019, HSK became the third largest language test brand after IELTS and TOEFL. The idea of "embracing the world and innovation" has always been the key to the continuous development of HSK.

I. Current Situation

In 2019, the Chinese proficiency test has grown as a global testing system of Chinese language with increasingly complete varieties and functions. It includes a series of Chinese language tests that are comprised of HSK, which plays a leading role, HSKK, YCT, BCT, and MCT, as well as a series of overseas Chinese language tests, including

Chinese classroom tests, mock/diagnostic Chinese tests and Chinese language tests for certificates[1]. In 1990, HSK was implemented for the first time, with 391 testees taking the test; in 2004, when the Confucius Institute was founded, the number of HSK test centers increased to 61 in 33 countries with 32,000 testees; the year of 2019 saw 1,229 Chinese language test centers in 150 countries, with 808,000 HSK testees and 7.5 million testees of various Chinese language tests.

This article analyzes the overall situation of HSK of 2019 with the data of 448,406 examinees participating in HSK1-6 exams in 2019 as samples (test reliability α: 0.905~0.941). The results show that HSK is developing rapidly, but there is an imbalance in distribution in the aspects of region, age and HSK level, which reflects the current situation of international Chinese language learning.

As for regional distribution, Asia (excluding China) accounted for 62.9% of HSK examinees in 2019, followed by Europe (8.9%), Africa (3.7%), North America (2.0%), South America (1.1%) and Oceania (0.5%), reflecting the uneven development of HSK. In 2019, there were seven countries with more than 10,000 testees and five countries with 5,000 to 10,000 testees (see Table 1). Except for well-known historical and cultural factors, the article makes statistical analysis on the number of testees from the 12 countries above (excluding China) by using the published number of international students in 2018 and the bilateral trade volume between the 12 countries and China. According to the result, "the number of international students in China" and "bilateral trade volume" were significantly positively correlated with the number of HSK testees ($p<0.001$), with R coefficients of 0.815 and 0.494 respectively.

1 At present, the overseas Chinese language tests authenticated by the Center for Language Education and Cooperation affiliated with the Ministry of Education of China include Oral Chinese Test (OCT) administered by Hong Kong and Chinese characters competence test (HNK) administered by South Korea.

Table 1 Statistics on the Number and Pass Rate of HSK Examinees in Some Countries in 2019

Country	Total Number	HSK 1		HSK 2		HSK 3		HSK 4		HSK 5		HSK 6	
		Number	Pass Rate	Number	Pass Rate	Number	Pass Rate	Number	Pass Rate	Number	Pass Rate	Number	Pass Rate
South Korea	102638	5233	95.26%	8349	93.75%	15313	79.66%	25319	66.84%	28261	62.25%	20163	64.82%
China	93738[1]	2265	95.01%	3896	92.35%	9997	80.59%	37411	64.76%	24630	70.01%	15539	66.74%
Thailand	50874	8194	71.15%	10826	70.76%	11431	57.96%	11556	51.22%	7697	47.84%	1170	55.13%
Japan	29836	2674	95.55%	4125	94.38%	6065	91.38%	6825	76.92%	6161	65.98%	3986	59.96%
Vietnam	21003	454	97.36%	2481	92.66%	6614	85.53%	6989	83.63%	3749	78.37%	716	72.07%
Indonesia	16612	3617	87.84%	4190	90.67%	3890	83.29%	3056	73.53%	1541	71.06%	318	77.99%
Myanmar	11947	1372	98.10%	2468	95.58%	2146	90.63%	2397	83.35%	1659	81.68%	1905	81.15%
The Philippines	11655	3789	65.29%	3250	66.58%	2870	55.16%	1155	41.30%	338	52.07%	253	77.47%
Russia	8162	1712	94.98%	1983	92.54%	1923	82.79%	1452	67.22%	934	56.96%	158	48.10%
Italy	6732	1945	94.91%	1927	95.23%	1365	81.90%	841	80.98%	439	72.67%	215	81.40%
France	5724	1344	94.20%	1798	88.38%	1484	70.96%	643	63.30%	328	66.46%	127	68.50%
Pakistan	5203	2598	77.60%	1425	77.33%	768	51.43%	315	33.33%	84	55.95%	13	15.38%
The United States	5120	931	87.86%	1007	90.07%	996	74.60%	1317	71.15%	645	69.46%	224	84.38%

(www.chinesetest.cn)

In terms of age distribution, the average age of HSK testees in 2019 is 21.71 years old and standard deviation is 7.97. The oldest is 88 years old and the youngest is 6 years old. 75% of them are younger than 24 years old (inclusive), and overall, testees are relatively young, showing a right-skewed distribution. The average age of HSK1 testees is 18.85, HSK2 19.36, HSK3 21.22, HSK4 22.37, HSK5 23.58, and HSK6 24.02. Besides, the average age of YCT testees is 12.88 years old, and 84% of YCT testees are under 15 (inclusive).

In light of the analysis of HSK scores and Chinese proficiency, HSK pass rate shows differences in terms of countries and HSK levels. Taking the 12 sample countries as an example, the pass rate of Myanmar, Vietnam, Italy and Indonesia is higher than the global average. Except HSK3 in the United States and HSK6 in Japan, the pass rates of other levels in the two countries are higher than the global average. As for HSK5-6, the pass

1 The examinees who take HSK in China are mainly foreign students and workers in China.

rate of France is higher than the global average, while that of Russia and South Korea is lower than the global average; the pass rates of the Philippines (except HSK6), Pakistan and Thailand are 9 to 50 percentage points lower than the global average. That reflects the differences of Chinese language education in various countries with respect to the historical tradition, the Chinese language level of students, teacher and curriculum quality, and the importance attached to by local governments. In addition, the pass rate of HSK decreases from 86.28% of HSK1 to 64.77% of HSK5, and the pass rate of HSK6 rises slightly to 67.13% (Figure 1), which basically conforms to the process of Chinese language learning and the gradient design of level test. But the reason for the rebound of the pass rate of HSK6 needs further study. In view of level distribution, lower-level tests are more popular overseas. HSK1-4 testees account for 70.06% of overall test takers, which proves that the Chinese proficiency of overseas learners is still generally at a medium or low level. The numbers of HSK3-5 testees rank top three, and that is probably related to the minimum requirement of Chinese language proficiency for studying in China and HSK4 or 5 is the common entry requirement of applying for Chinese colleges and universities.

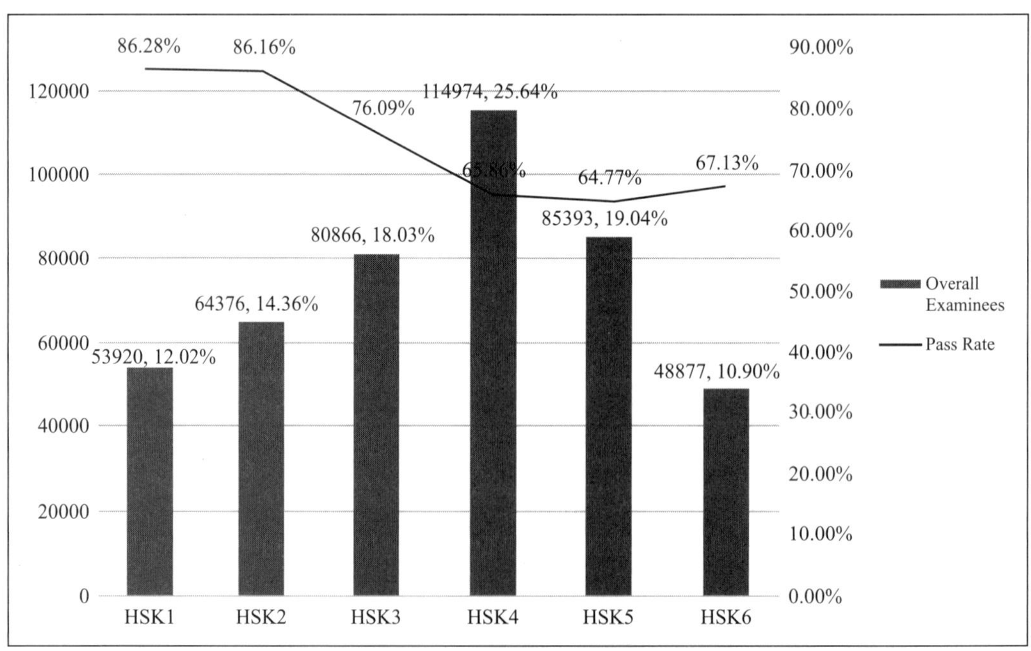

(www.chinesetest.cn)

Figure 1 The Number and Pass Rate of HSK Examinees at All Levels in 2019

II. Development Philosophy

1. Being Student-Centered

With the increasing number of examinees participating in Chinese language tests, a "student-centered" approach to the test development has vigorously promoted the Chinese language teaching and learning: first, the Chinese language test is an important means of assessing Chinese language learning, not only based on the learning outcomes, but also on the learning processes and phases. It helps Chinese language learners improve their learning by making up for their deficiencies. In 2019, 6.7 million Chinese learners took part in classroom tests and diagnostic/mock tests; second, in designing tests and courses, we strive to create an authentic Chinese learning environment and encourage learners to "put what they learn into practice". In 2019, HSK covers 47 topics in 10 subjects, including "daily life, occupations and work, education and culture, science and nature", comprehensively demonstrating various scenarios of people's lives and Chinese society. More than 1.25 million people have learned the courses based on these topics; third, HSK has built a bridge for learners to link China to the rest of the world. According to incomplete statistics, 150,000 foreigners learned about China through HSK Study Abroad and Employment Exhibition, 398,000 international students studied in China and more than 500,000 foreigners worked in China in 2019 after passing HSK proficiency tests.

2. Highlighting Chinese Language Features

Scholars generally agree that linguistic competence is extremely complex and abstract. In 2019, Zhang Houcan pointed out the abstract "linguistic competence" always embodies in the specific "language proficiency" in specific time and space. Take HSK as an example. It describes the language competence through the descriptions of language proficiency in six levels and each level in three dimensions: Chinese vocabulary, subjects and topics as well as grammar function. For instance, HSK1 requires learners to master 150 words, 3 subjects, 15 topics, 8 language tasks, and 40 grammar points; HSK6 learners need to master more than 5,000 words, 9 subjects, 47 topics, 14 language tasks, and 23 grammar points, all of which embody the fundamental features of Chinese language. In the new era, the Chinese language test development continues highlighting the features of Chinese language and more accurately describes the Chinese proficiency of second language learners from more dimensions. The book describing the new Chinese language teaching and testing standards, *Chinese Proficiency Grading Standards for International Chinese Language Education,* was released[1]. The *Standards* highlights the features of Chinese language in the three stages of novice, intermediate, and advanced with nine levels. The *Standards* uses four basic elements of the Chinese language: syllables, characters, vocabulary, and grammar, to form a "four-dimensional conception" (1,110 syllables, 3,000 Chinese characters, 11,092 words and 572 grammatical rules) and verbal communicative competence, topic task content, and quantitative linguistic indices to form three evaluation dimensions, and makes Chinese listening, speaking, reading, writing as well as translating and interpreting, the five language skills, to accurately determine the Chinese proficiency of learners. In the future, the *Standards* will guide the teaching, learning, testing, and evaluation of international Chinese language in a unified manner to adapt to the trend of international Chinese language education development in the new era.

3. Powered by Scientific Research and Artificial Intelligence

All Chinese proficiency tests always adhere to the idea of "science and technology is the first productive force". First, in 2019, we continued to set up 17 "Hankao international scientific research fund projects" to promote basic research and technology development, and took the lead in two key projects of the State Language Commission of China. Second, the international Chinese proposition platform and digital question bank system encrypted 120,000 Chinese test questions in six years of efficient operation through the "cloud proposition" mode of network proposition and intelligent test paper generation. Third, by the end of 2019, 489 online examination sites have been

1 *Chinese Proficiency Grading Standards for International Chinese Language Education* was released in March, 2021, and was officially implemented as the standard of State Language Commission on July 1, 2021.

set up around the world by using network cloud platform technology, with an online examination coverage rate of 40%; on the basis of remote marking and machine marking, HSK online simulation diagnosis system was launched to automatically diagnose Chinese level and learning deficiency, and help Chinese learners improve their learning methods. 15,775 people used the system that year. Fourth, in 2019, in addition to traditional e-mail registration and examination consultation, multilingual smart customer service "Xiaoneng" was widely used, and 11,940 messages were automatically replied throughout the year; face recognition technology was introduced to identify candidates so as to ensure the fairness and safety of the examination.

III. International Cooperation

With the widespread use of Chinese language and the increasing number of learners in the world, some national or international education organizations have formulated Chinese language test standards, and some countries have incorporated Chinese into their national education systems, implemented Chinese language tests, and even set Chinese language as a subject of their "national college entrance examination". Those Chinese language tests meet the diverse needs of Chinese learners around the world, and they have become an important member of the Chinese language testing family, complementing HSK and other Chinese proficiency tests.

1. Alignment of International Standards

In order to better serve Chinese language learners around the world, the sponsors, implementors, and partners of Chinese language tests will continue to cooperate with international education institutions and education authorities of various countries to promote the alignment of different Chinese language test standards and the reciprocal authentication of *Chinese Proficiency Grading Standards for International Chinese Language Education*.

2. Authentication of Tests

Chinese proficiency test actively cooperates with the professional testing institutions of various countries to carry out two-way authentication of Chinese language tests. HSK and Chinese Characters Proficiency Test (HNK administered in South Korea) conducted two-way authentication for 2,591 testees in 2019. HSK and Sijil Pelajaran Malaysia (SPM) conducted a trial test on 739 testees for future reciprocal authentication. In the future, we will carry out two-way authentication of Chinese language tests with more countries and regions.

Language is the bridge and bond of communication. As the demand for learning Chinese in various countries continues to grow, more foreigners will learn about China and experience Chinese culture through learning Chinese language, which will surely drive the scale of HSK to expand continuously. Benefited from the guidance and practice of "being student-centered", "highlighting Chinese language features", and "powered by scientific research and artificial intelligence", Chinese language test has met the demand of learning Chinese in various countries and ensured the quality of international Chinese language education. In the future, the Chinese language test will further play a role in constantly improving the standards as well as evaluation system of Chinese teaching and learning to make them more scientific, open, and easy to implement so that the test will be an effective tool for grading and classifying Chinese language teaching which caters to different students. The test will also ensure the continuous improvement of the quality of international Chinese language education.

(Li Peize, Huang Lei, Li Lingyu, Xiao Yuan & Xie Nini,
Chinese Testing International Co., Ltd.)

Report on the Development of Confucius Institutes

Confucius Institutes are non-profit education institutions co-constructed by China and other countries to accommodate to the global need of Chinese language learning, strengthening the understanding of Chinese language and culture for international communities, enhancing the education communication and cooperation between China and other countries, and promoting multi-cultural development and building a harmonious world. Over the years, Confucius Institutes (CIs) have become international language learning institutions with global recognition through conducting Chinese language teaching around the world in training Chinese language teachers, providing Chinese language teaching resources and information about China's education and culture, administering Chinese language tests and Certificate for Teachers of Chinese to Speakers of Other Languages. Based on the statistics reported by the Center for Language Education and Cooperation of the Ministry of Education, this report gives an analytic review of the development of Confucius Institutes in 2019.

I. Institution Setting

1. Overall Situation

Confucius Institutes, as non-profit educational institutions set up by Chinese universities and overseas partnership universities to help people from all countries or regions to learn Chinese language and understand Chinese culture, are the bridges of language communication, cultural understanding, and mutual learning between civilizations. Confucius Institutes have provided a good platform and contributed to encouraging cultural and people-to-people exchanges between China and foreign countries, promoting the development of Chinese language teaching overseas, and facilitating the interactions of diverse cultures and people-to-people contacts.

It has been more than 15 years since the first Confucius Institute was established in 2004. As of 2010, over 300 Confucius Institutes had been established, and in the following five years, Confucius Institutes expanded rapidly at an annual growth rate of around 40%. The total number of Confucius Institutes exceeded 500 in 2015, and has entered a period of steady development since then. In the second five-year period, the growth in quantity gradually slowed down, whereas the high-quality internal development became the primary task (as shown in Figure 1).

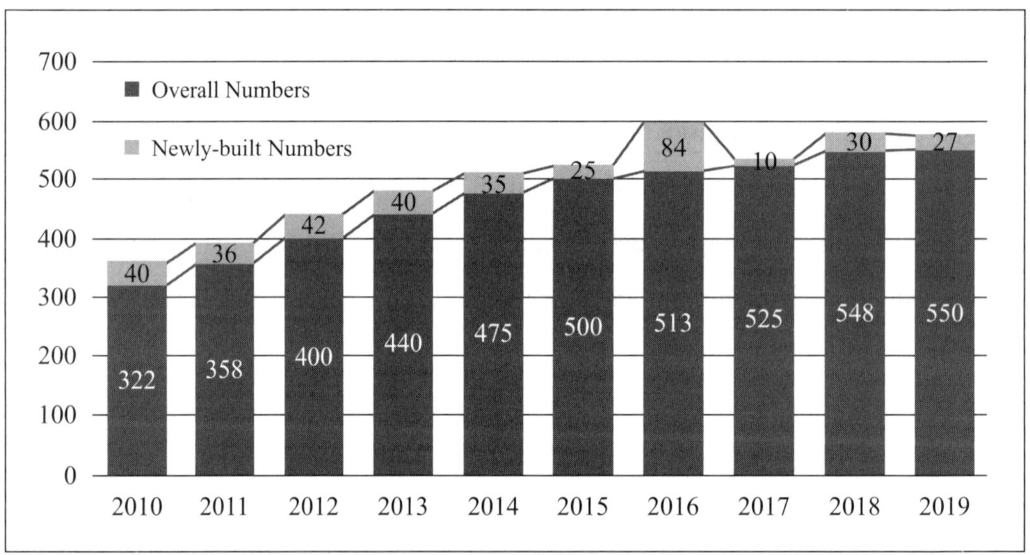

Source: Chinese International Education Foundation

Figure 1 Construction of Confucius Institutes in 2010-2019

In recent years, diversification has become an important feature of the development of Confucius Institutes: (1) Partnerships are diversified. Unlike language promotion institutes of other countries, one of the main features of Confucius Institutes is that they are operated through Sino-foreign joint cooperation, with partnership agencies of schools, governments, enterprises and social organizations. (2) The benefit groups are diversified. The target groups of Confucius Institutes include students, teachers, experts and scholars, industry elites and ordinary people in communities, and these benefit groups range from different age groups to various professions. Thus, Confucius Institutes have developed diversified features in practice for different partnerships in order to meet the diversified needs of their benefit groups.

2. Regional Features

In 2011—2019, the regional development of Confucius Institutes/Classrooms has the following features:

(1) In Europe, Confucius Institutes keep their highest level in terms of the number, and the number of Confucius Classrooms is relatively moderate, both of which maintain a high growth rate.

(2) In the Americas, the number of Confucius Institutes is also kept at a high level, comparable to that in Europe; the number of Confucius Classrooms ranks the top, more than the sum of other regions, despite occasional decrease in growth.

(3) In Asia, the number of Confucius Institutes is in the middle of the ranking, but is growing rapidly; the number of Confucius Classrooms is in the lower middle of the ranking with a steady increase.

(4) In Africa, the number of Confucius Institutes and Confucius Classrooms is in the lower-middle range, but they have been developing rapidly in recent years.

(5) Due to the limited number of countries in the Oceania region, the number of Confucius Institutes and Confucius Classrooms there ranks the bottom, but their development is significant.

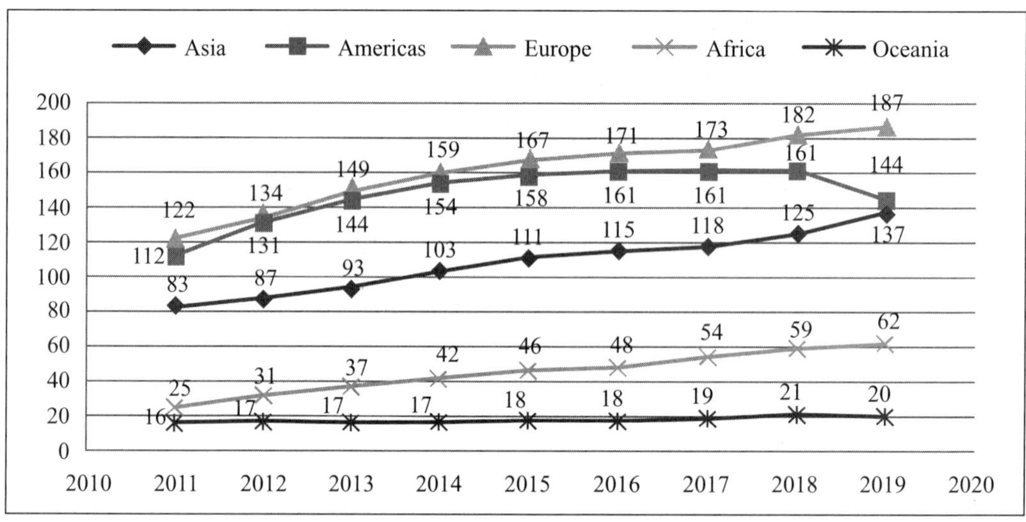

Figure 2　Regional Distribution of Confucius Institutes

On the whole, the development of Confucius Institutes or Confucius Classrooms in Europe and the Americas has been through ups and downs, but the local demand for international Chinese language education is still huge, and cooperation and exchange are still the mainstream; Asia and Oceania have generally developed more steadily, and specialized Confucius Institutes or Confucius Classrooms have been set up according to

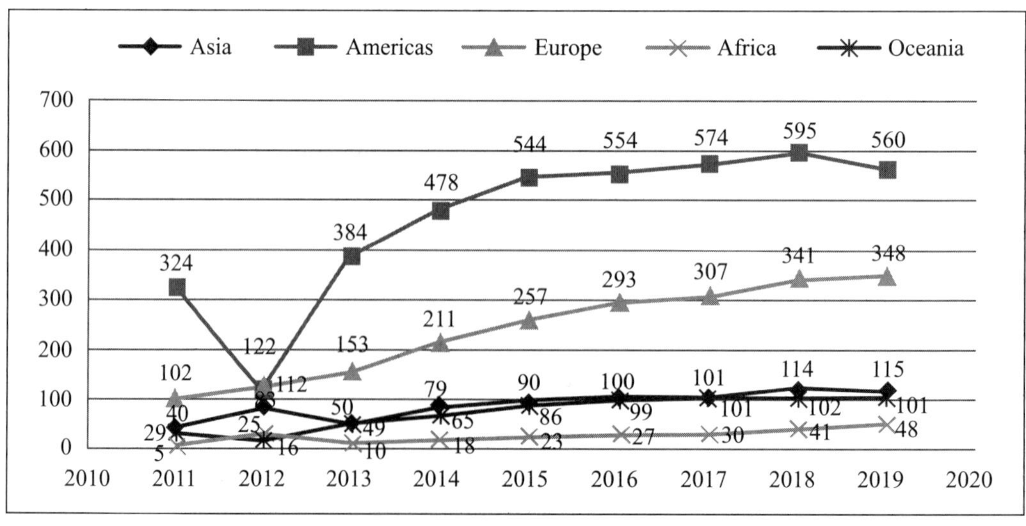

Figure 3　Regional Distribution of Confucius Classrooms

the local special needs; Africa and China have close contacts in politics, economy and trade, but language and cultural exchanges still fall short and should become the focus of future development.

In 2019, the distribution of Confucius Institutes and Confucius Classrooms is as follows: 550 Confucius Institutes are located in 152 countries (regions), including 137 in 37 countries (regions) in Asia, accounting for 25%; 62 in 45 countries (regions) in Africa, accounting for 11%; 187 in 41 countries (regions) in Europe, accounting for 34%; 144 in 24 countries (regions) in Americas, accounting for 26%; and 20 in 5 countries (regions) in Oceania, accounting for 4%. There are 1,172 Confucius Classrooms in 93 countries (regions), including 115 in 24 countries (regions) in Asia, accounting for 10%; 48 in 20 countries (regions) in Africa, accounting for 4%; 348 in 31 countries (regions) in Europe, accounting for 30%; 560 in 13 countries (regions) in Americas, accounting for 48%; and 101 in 5 countries (regions) in Oceania, accounting for 8%. The number of students receiving face-to-face instruction in Confucius Institutes totaled 1.81 million, five times that of 2009. The number of online students reached 1,688,000, double that of 2018. It can be seen that the paths for learners to learn Chinese are diversified and the teaching methods are becoming more plentiful, and the Confucius Institutes, through continuous development and construction, can better meet the individualized learning needs of learners.

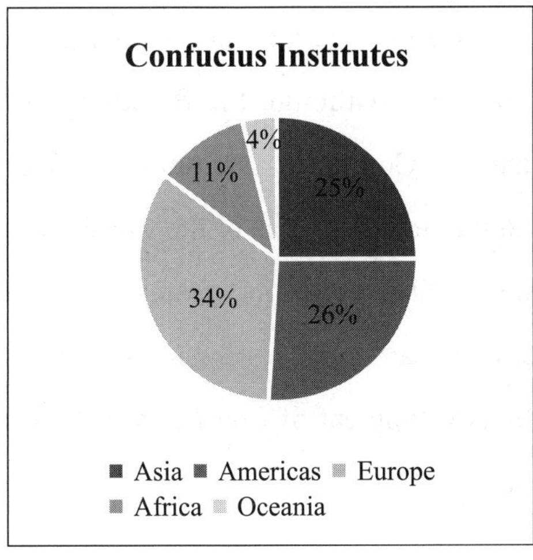

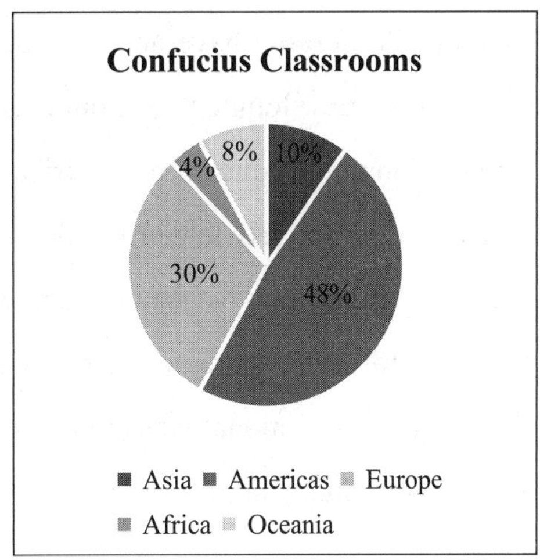

Figure 4 Regional Distribution of Confucius Institutes and Confucius Classrooms in 2019

From the data, we can see Confucius Institutes and Confucius Classrooms in Europe and the Americas still account for two-thirds of the total number, while the number in Asia is now close to that of the Americas, showing a latecomer's surpassing momentum; the development in Africa is also beginning to show its scale.

Since Confucius Institutes initiated its Model Confucius Institute program in 2013, 48 Model Confucius Institutes have been built worldwide, 19 of which are in Europe. Up to 2019, the UK has established 30 Confucius Institutes and 165 Confucius Classrooms in primary and secondary schools, relatively accounting for 5.5% and 14.0% of all Confucius Institutes and Confucius Classrooms worldwide respectively, ranking first in Europe and second in the world.

Notably, in recent years, Confucius Institutes face dilemma in Europe and the United States. With an increasing attention to Confucius Institutes from Western media, misunderstanding is growing too. Negative comments due to misunderstandings have been on the rise since 2014. The misunderstandings mainly arise from the biased conceptions of the aims, impact and prospects of Confucius Institutes. Some censures disrupted the operation of local Confucius Institutes. However, the development of Confucius Institutes/Classrooms in Asia and Africa is promising. With a long history and solid foundation of Chinese language education in Asia as well as the ever-growing demand from the countries and regions along the "Belt and Road", specialized programs such as "Chinese +" have accommodated the new need of the Confucius Institutes'/Classrooms' development in Southeast Asian countries. Although the foundation of Chinese language education in Africa is weak and the Confucius Institutes in Africa account for a relatively low proportion compared to that in other areas of the world, 80% of African countries have set up Confucius Institutes with more distinct features in each country. Moreover, there are increasing calls from African countries for incorporating Chinese into the national education system and the development of Confucius Institutes in Africa is gaining momentum towards a bright future.

II. Teaching Modes

1. Chinese Language Curriculum Landing Project

In order to meet the demand for standardized Chinese language teaching content in the countries around the world, Confucius Institute Headquarters/Hanban promulgated *International Curriculum for Chinese Language Education* in 2008 which was translated into 45 languages in the following five years, providing guidance for Confucius Institutes (Classrooms) around the world and various types of Chinese language teaching in the schools and universities abroad. The *Curriculum* presents a comprehensive review and detailed description of the objectives and content of Chinese as a second language course, aiming to provide reference and standards for Chinese language teaching institutions and teachers in the formulation of teaching plans, assessment of learner's language competence, and development of teaching materials. To accommodate the new changes in Chinese language teaching and draw upon the research results in a timely manner, the revision of the *Curriculum* was launched in 2013 to better plan and guide the design of Chinese language teaching courses, the development of textbooks, and the assessment of Chinese language proficiency.

In order to successfully incorporate Chinese language education into the national education systems in more countries and achieve the goal of localizing Chinese language education internationally, as well as to address the issue that the *International Curriculum for Chinese Language Education* cannot be directly implemented overseas, the Division of Confucius Institute Development of Beijing Language and Culture University has taken the *Curriculum* as its core guide, selected key countries with typical features from all over the world, and integrated the *Curriculum* into their national foreign language curriculum plan with the country-oriented and practical features of the actual teaching of Chinese language in their local primary and secondary schools. Through overseas governmental educational institutions, we closely combine China's established Chinese language teaching standards, teaching modes, teaching methods and teaching resources with overseas Chinese language teaching systems.

By the end of 2019, the project has been carried out in ten countries on six continents: the United States and Canada in North America, Chile in South America, Spain and Bulgaria in Europe, New Zealand in Oceania, Cameroon and Zambia in Africa, and Thailand and Kyrgyzstan in Asia. Some outcomes have been achieved so far, including *Chinese Language Curriculum of Elementary Grades (K-5) in the US*, *Curriculum of Secondary Grades 6-12 in the US*, *Chinese Language Curriculum of Middle School Grades (1-4) in Chile*, *Curriculum for Chinese Language Education in Cameroon Middle School Grades 3&4*, *Chinese Task-based Curriculum L1-8*, and *Chinese Language Curriculum for Secondary Schools in Zambia*.

The overseas landing project of integrating *International Curriculum for Chinese Language Education* into overseas countries' curricula for foreign language education complied with the foreign language/Chinese language teaching requirements of the target countries, adhered to the scientific system and core contents of the *Curriculum* and adopted the national popular modes of compilation, which are well-received and officially authorized by primary and secondary schools. The Chinese language curriculum/syllabus will be included in the national foreign language education systems as a sub-level guideline to ensure that overseas Chinese learners, especially primary and secondary school students, can learn Chinese language in a more scientific and systematic way in their own education system and feel the charm of Chinese culture. The successful landing of *International Curriculum for Chinese Language Education* will help cultivate an affinity with China and Chinese culture among the new generation overseas by osmosis so as to help build a positive image of China in the world and increase China's international influence.

2. Confucius Institute Online

Confucius Institute Online (www.chinesecio.com) is a web-based remote Chinese online teaching system built by the Confucius Institute Headquarters in 2008, aiming to make full use of new technologies and new modes, such as the Internet, big data and artificial intelligence to implement Internet teaching programs, build an online learning platform for Chinese language learners around the world, and provide more resources for Chinese culture lovers. Confucius Institute Online currently has more than 5,500 MOOCs and micro-lectures in 143 courses in 7 categories, including Chinese language learning, Chinese language tests, an overview of China, traditional culture, teacher training, vocational Chinese language, and lectures by experts, which are an integrated system for on-demand classes, livestream classes, interactive teaching, intelligent teaching tools, and course management, providing a multi-level service system of teaching, learning, examinations, and training to best meet the needs of all Chinese language learners to learn anytime and anywhere.

By the end of 2019, Confucius Institute Online has had 1,688,000 registered students, with 12.02 million visits in total, over 4,000 teachers offering more than 300,000 online classes, with over 7,000 courseware available online. For instance, the "Chinese 900" website also provides learners with resources in 19 languages, including English, French, Russian, Spanish, Korean, Japanese, Arabic and Burmese, etc. to facilitate international Chinese language learners.

3. "Chinese +" Program

In recent years, with the diversification of the demand for Chinese language talents in various countries, the objectives, contents and modes of teaching Chinese language in Confucius Institutes have also started to change. As more and more countries need "Chinese + technology", "Chinese + commerce and trade" and other versatile talents, Confucius Institutes have timely launched a series of "Chinese +" special programs to help countries cultivate versatile talents.

For example, the Confucius Institute at Kansai Gaidai University in Japan offered a course on "Chinese Language for Flight Attendants" starting 2017. It is aimed at Kansai Gaidai University (KUFS) students who have passed HSK Level 4 or higher and intend to work in the aviation field in future. The pilot course had 30 places per semester, and as soon as it was launched, the places were all taken. By the fall semester of 2019, the course had launched for three consecutive years and six semesters, and the number of the class had increased from one to two, with more than 180 students participating in the course. At the same time, the Confucius Institute closely focused on the career theme, linking Chinese language learning with employment, and had successively added special Chinese courses, such as Business Chinese, Medical Chinese, and Global Career Planning Studies.

The 2019 International Chinese Language Education Conference also set up "Chinese + vocational skills" forum for the first time, and invited Chinese and foreign enterprises and experts in education to discuss how to match employment and entrepreneurship. Participants expressed their views and had a heated discussion on the sustainable development of the "Chinese +" program. At present, more than 100 Confucius Institutes in more than 40 countries around the world offer "Chinese +" courses in dozens of fields, such as high-speed railway, business and trade, and aviation. In the future, this program will provide more Chinese vocational education opportunities for students from different countries through continuous innovation and development.

III. Multi-lingual Periodicals

Confucius Institute is a series of publications sponsored by the Confucius Institute Headquarters/Hanban. The first edition of *Confucius Institute* in Chinese and English was launched in March 2009. In order to further enrich the content, expand the international perspective and meet the diversified needs of learning Chinese language and understanding Chinese culture in different countries, a bilingual version of *Confucius Institute* in 10 languages, including Spanish, French, Russian, Arabic, German, Portuguese, Italian, Japanese, Korean, Thai and other languages paired with Chinese version has been launched since 2010. By the end of 2019, about 200,000 copies of each issue of *Confucius Institute* in all these languages were distributed globally, seven times more than its initial distribution. Its distribution has reached to more than 160 countries and regions with an increase of 20 countries in 2018 and 40 countries in 2014 and its readership over 1 million. *Confucius Institute* has been presented at the Frankfurt Book

Fair, Languages Expo in Paris, Morocco International Language Festival and other top international exhibitions for many times, and has been noted and welcomed by most local people of other countries.

Confucius Institute mainly showcases Chinese culture, activities of Confucius Institutes, Chinese language teaching and learning, and tells stories of people-to-people and cultural exchanges between China and foreign countries. As the only publication in China with independent ISSN in multiple language versions and local edition, publication and distribution, *Confucius Institute* is a distinct periodical "going global", facilitating cross-cultural communication with vivid teaching materials for people from all over the world to learn Chinese language and understand China. In 2016, it was selected as one of "the top 100 most beautiful periodicals" by China Periodicals Association, China Periodical Yearbook and China Periodicals Fair. In 2017, among 11 bilingual magazines presented at the Frankfurt Book Fair for the first time with "China's Magazines" organized by the State Administration of Press, Publication, Radio, Film and Television, *Confucius Institute* received enthusiastic praise and positive feedback. While hailed as a printed periodical "going global", *Confucius Institute* actively explores media integration and transformation, and creates "Internet +" online interactive operation mode, through the integration of the *Confucius Institute*'s website, the WeChat official account and its APP, to make possible "one release, multi-platform display", and "printed publications as main body, website and new media as two wings".

In 2019, Confucius Institute continued to maintain a good and steady development, with more diversified modes of operation and teaching on the basis of focusing on the main task of Chinese language education. At present, Confucius Institutes are in a critical period of internal development, deep integration and brand enhancement. In the future, we will focus on language as the main task, actively accommodate to the (overseas) local communities and strengthen its educational nature. Meanwhile, we will make efforts to improve the quality and efficiency of Confucius Institutes by expanding the sources of funds and resources and advancing the reform of the institutional mechanism. Through policy guidance and coordination, we support the upgrading and transformation of

Confucius Institutes as a whole, and promote market-oriented operation of Confucius Institutes as a global education brand for public good through the establishment of international private foundations and the center for language communication and cooperation. Through such transformation and upgrading mechanism, Confucius Institute can further achieve its sustainable localized development.

Looking ahead, Confucius Institutes will significantly supplement the degree programs of Bachelor, Master and Doctorate for international Chinese language education, and support Chinese universities and colleges to establish international Chinese language teacher colleges. Policies of improving the welfare of Chinese language teachers and volunteer teachers sent abroad will be formulated jointly with relevant departments. Support will be provided for Chinese and foreign experts to jointly implement high-quality textbooks projects, improve and specify the series of standards for TCSOL, and refine the standards for international Chinese language teacher qualifications; Confucius Institutes will continue to support and encourage the active participation of various schools, enterprises, social organizations and individuals in China and other countries, especially their participation in the construction of Confucius Institutes and international Chinese language education through co-founding foundations or other means, to ensure Confucius Institutes continue playing a major role in international Chinese language teaching to its fullest.

(Chen Lixia, Beijing Language and Culture University)

III Regional Reports

Report on the Development of International Chinese Language Teaching in Asia

I. Overall Situation

International Chinese language education of 2019 in Asia can be described with two keywords: "hot" and "new". "Hot" implies Chinese language continuously gains more popularity; "new" indicates the innovative breakthroughs international Chinese language education have achieved by improving quality and efficiency, and through transformation and upgrading. These features are as follow:

1. Continuous Increase of the Countries Incorporating Chinese Language into the National Education System

By the end of 2019, 69 countries and regions around the world have officially incorporated Chinese language as an important subject into their national education systems by formulating policies and regulations. Some countries have listed Chinese language as one of the foreign language subjects in university entrance exams and others have placed Chinese language throughout foreign language education system from pre-school to higher education. Incorporating Chinese language into the national education system gives full expression to the international status of Chinese language and prioritizes the improvement of Chinese language system standards on the agenda.

In 2019, following Japan, South Korea, the Philippines, Thailand, Malaysia and

Singapore, Saudi Arabia, the United Arab Emirates (UAE), Georgia and other countries have announced their incorporation of Chinese language into their educational systems for the first time. Saudi Arabia made the announcement on February 23rd that Chinese language would be incorporated into the curriculum of all educational stages in order to make education more diversified; the UAE announced that about 60 public schools from kindergartens to high schools would officially launch Chinese language courses starting from September of 2019. Meanwhile, the UAE Ministry of Education also planned to recruit 150 Chinese language teachers in the academic year 2019-2020 and expanded Chinese language teaching to 200 public schools; in early 2019, China and Georgia signed a *Memorandum of Cooperation on Promoting Chinese Language Education in Tbilisi*, officially confirming the incorporation of Chinese language teaching into the national education system of Georgia.

2. New Addition and Establishment of Confucius Institutes and Confucius Classrooms

As Confucius Institutes (CIs) continuously expand in scope, new CIs have been established and added in the countries along the "Belt and Road". By 2019, 137 CIs have been established in 37 countries in Asia with 115 Confucius Classrooms constructed in 24 countries.

The year of 2019 witnessed the establishment of 27 CIs and 66 Confucius Classrooms, including 4 in Asia: namely Chinese Language Center at Pyongyang Foreign Languages University in North Korea, Chinese Language Center at Villa Maria Academy High School in Maldives, the Confucius Institute at the University of Jeddah in Saudi Arabia, and the Confucius Classroom at Timor-Leste Business School in the Democratic Republic of Timor-Leste. At the International Conference on Chinese Language Education in December of 2019, Indonesia, the Philippines, Georgia, Saudi Arabia, Maldives, and Timor-Leste attended the signing ceremonies for new Confucius Institutes and Confucius Classrooms.

3. The Increasing Number of Chinese Language Learners

In 2019, China's GDP reached $14 trillion, making it the world's second largest economy. The rapid development of the economy and the steady increase in comprehensive national power has led to a growing demand for Chinese language talents from overseas. Meanwhile, more Asian countries are participating in the "Belt and Road" Initiative, which further promotes the development of international Chinese language education.

In 2019, the rigid demand for learning Chinese language continues to increase, with the number of learners reaching record highs, and Chinese language learners worldwide has exceeded 150 million. There are more than 60 thousand Chinese learners in Malaysia. In 2019, the Confucius Institute at the University of Malaya alone enrolled 12,000 students. In terms of the number of Chinese learners, Thailand has more than 1 million, Japan has exceeded 2 million, and South Korea has exceeded 10 million, the highest in the world.

Taking an overview of Chinese language learners, there are several distinctive features: (1) The purpose of learning Chinese language is more for professional development than simply as a personal hobby and the learners have more awareness of improving language competence for their career development. Thus, more rigid demand for Chinese language provision is on the rise. (2) The demand is more prominent for "Chinese +", especially the massive demand for "Chinese + vocational skills". That indicates a more practical need in Asia for cultivating "Chinese +" versatile talents, especially "Chinese + vocational skills". (3) Learners' age is getting lower with an increasing number of learners in primary and secondary schools and even kindergartens. (4) The number of online learners is on the rise, and they show much interest in the smart products for Chinese language learning.

4. Expanding Chinese Language Teaching Institutions and Diversified Operation Modes

"Mandarin fever" has triggered the extreme prosperity of education market. For example, Chinese language education in South Korea, Thailand and other countries has expanded from universities to primary and secondary schools and even kindergartens, which make differentiated learning more distinctive in terms of school levels and age groups; institutions offer Chinese courses to universities, primary and secondary schools, vocational schools and private training schools; in addition to learning Chinese language, there is a surging demand for learning Chinese plus subjects and vocational skills in a both professional and personalized way; learning modes range from in-person group learning and one-on-one coaching to online learning, some taking daytime classes, some attending evening tutoring classes. The ever-growing learners have resulted in the expansion of enrollment in existing teaching institutions and stimulated a number of new institutions to come into being.

The diversity of learning needs has led to an increasing diversification of schooling modes, with some schools adopting a variety of ways to deliver courses such as through joint partnerships and school-enterprise cooperation to provide better development opportunities for learners. Notably, "Chinese + vocational skills" has made rapid progress in 2019. For example, the Confucius Institute at Kathmandu University in Nepal has held a "Chinese + vehicle maintenance and repair" training course from March to May; the Confucius Institute at University of Tehran in Iran has offered a "Chinese + vocational skills" training course; the Confucius Institute at University of Malaya in Malaysia has cooperated with Maybank, Petronas, the Ministry of Home Affairs (Malaysia), Royal Malaysian Police, the Immigration Department and so on to offer series of special courses like "Chinese + policing", "Chinese + law", "Chinese + commerce" and "Airport Customs Chinese", and on November 14th, 2019, the Confucius Institute has cooperated with ZTE Education Management Co. to offer the "Vocational Chinese language training class" for communication, Internet of Things, big data and other socially desirable programs; vocational schools in Thailand cooperated with their counterparts in China to train talents in the mode of "Chinese + vocational skills", which gains more popularity among the Thai learners. The government also hopes that vocational skills training can be assessed and certified.

5. Remarkable Improvement of Teaching Quality and Efficiency

In light of the huge body of learners, it is particularly important in international Chinese language education to improve teaching quality and set up a sound standard system for Chinese language teaching in 2019.

The problems from the "three Ts", namely, teachers, teaching materials and teaching methods, have been under exploration since the beginning of TCSOL when foreign students – mainly from other Asian countries – came to China to learn Chinese. After decades of research work, and due to the similarities shared by Asian cultures, as well as the frequent contacts and exchanges brought by globalization, the "three Ts" issue in the aspect of teaching international students in China is addressed properly; but in overseas countries, especially in those countries with a large number of Chinese language learners, the issue of the "three Ts" is still prominent and in a state of spiral upward development on the whole.

In the aspect of Chinese language teacher provision overseas, there are two sources: either sent from China or trained locally overseas. Specialized and localized faculty are the mainstay of teacher training in 2019 and beyond. In 2019, Hanban alone has provided 5,885 new teaching positions for volunteer Chinese teachers. Some Chinese universities and colleges have hosted training sessions for volunteer Chinese teachers: for example, at the end of 2018, Beijing Language and Culture University held the Confucius Institute Headquarters/Hanban 2019 pre-service training for 307 volunteer Chinese teachers, who were from 94 institutions in 27 provinces, before being sent to teach in primary and secondary schools in South Korea; on March 21st of 2019, Hainan Normal University conducted Confucius Institute Headquarters/Hanban training for 100 volunteer teachers to Thailand. Some countries also focused on training local Chinese language teachers in 2019. For example, the University of Malaya of Malaysia set up a postgraduate program in TCSOL, which was co-built by the University's Graduate School, the School of Languages, the School of Education, the Confucius Institute and Beijing Foreign Studies University, aiming to cultivate local Chinese language teachers for Malaysia in urgent need. In December 2019, more than 50 Nepalese local Chinese language teachers came to Beijing International Chinese College to participate in the 2019 Nepalese Local Chinese Language Teachers Training Class in China. With nearly 5 million Chinese language teachers worldwide, the overall capacity of teachers has been certainly improved, however, despite all means, the demand for teachers from various countries is still larger than the supply.

In terms of teaching materials, while traditional textbooks continue to play their roles, constructing localized and compiling "Chinese +" textbooks become heated topics. Under the guidance of developing standardized, localized and diversified Chinese language textbooks, new progress has been made in the development of standardized textbooks for overseas Chinese language teaching and cooperation in the development of localized textbooks by China with other countries. After integrating Chinese language into its national education system in 2019, the UAE starts to use the textbook co-authored by the UAE Ministry of Education and Hanban. The UAE is also working with Hanban to continuously develop a set of cultural textbooks that will help UAE students better understand all aspects of Chinese society.

In terms of teaching modes and methods, in-person teaching is still the mainstream, but the new technology taps into and promotes online teaching. The interactive teaching mode of online and in-person teaching is emerging, and the construction of online teaching resources is of immediate urgency. In teaching, teachers consciously pay more attention to a variety of teaching modes and methods accommodating to the local culture and the clients. Task-based language teaching, thematic teaching, situational approach, activity approach, experiential teaching and other diversified teaching methods are popular and with good effects.

6. Record Highs of HSK Test Takers

The number of Chinese Proficiency Test (HSK) testees reached a record high in Asia. In Sri Lanka, 102 applicants took the first HSK and HSKK tests held by Confucius Institute at University of Kelaniya on January 12. In Myanmar, the first HSK in 2019 organized by Fuxing Confucius Classroom on May 11 attracted 1,058 testees. In Thailand, 506 students from Kwangtong School and Kamphaeng Phet School applied for the first HSK test held by Kwangtong School in 2019 with the highest number ever. On February 24th, the second HSK, HSKK and YCT held by the Confucius Institute at Bansomdejchaopraya Rajabhat University in 2019 attracted 1,420 testees. In 2019, a total of 12,327 students participated in the HSK at Phuket Confucius Institute, ranking first among all the Confucius Institutes in Thailand. In Vietnam, the first HSK was organized by the Confucius Institute at Hanoi University in January of 2020 and 1,250 students took the test. In Japan, 34,108 testees took the HSK in 2018, and the surge remained in 2019. For example, in the second HSK on July 13th of 2019 held by the Confucius Institute at Kansai Gaidai University in Japan, 884 people registered for the test and 867 finally took the test, both figures setting record highs.

II. Cases of Chinese Language Education in Different Countries —Thailand and South Korea

1. TCSOL in Thailand

Chinese language has risen to become the second most popular foreign language in Thailand because it has incorporated into the national education system of Thailand much earlier. There are 16 Confucius Institutes and 20 Confucius Classrooms in Thailand, with a total of over 17,000 volunteer Chinese teachers in more than 1,000 universities, primary and secondary schools in 73 provinces. Chinese language education in Thailand continues to gain rapid momentum in 2019, with 3,500 schools offering Chinese language courses, 6,500 local and Chinese language teachers of other nationalities, and 890,000 students learning Chinese language.

In 2019, the following are notable features of TCSOL in Thailand:

(1) Ever-growing Demand for "Chinese + Vocational Skills"

The "Belt and Road" Initiative, EEC (Eastern Economic Corridor), China-Thailand high-speed railway under construction, etc. have provided more job opportunities for young people in Thailand, and more teenagers, especially vocational school students, want to learn both a skill and Chinese language. Thus, these have fueled a surge in "Chinese + vocational skills" education market. In order to meet the market demand, the Vocational Education Institute in Thailand has compiled the local textbook *Communication Chinese*. In addition, China and Thailand jointly conducted training programs. For example, in August 2019, 69 Thai students participated in the "Tianjin Municipal Government Scholarship Program for Vocational Education in Thailand" under the "Vocational Chinese Language Talents Training Plan in Thailand" at Tianjin Normal University and achieved a successful completion.

(2) A Record High Number of HSK Testees

HKS has demonstrated a brand effect in Thailand, and the number of testees has reached a record high of over 100,000. On April 27th of 2019, the 2019 Chinese Language Test Conference in Thailand was held in Bangkok. More than 50 directors and test directors from 23 Confucius Institutes (Classrooms) and test centers in Thailand attended the conference. In 2019, 10,185 testees have taken HSK at Phuket Confucius Institute, which exceeded 10,000 for the first time. In 2019, the Confucius Institute at Chiang Mai University organized 92 HSK at 23 testing centers with 10,059 testees and there were 2,021 testees in its affiliated Chong Hua Freshman Confucius Classrooms with another record high. Chinese proficiency tests in the Confucius Institute at Chiang Mai University mainly fall into three types: HSK, YCT and HSKK, with testees of all ages ranging from children to the elderly.

(3) Unprecedented Emphasis on Teacher Education

On the one hand, volunteer Chinese teachers are selected within China, and as of 2019, China has sent a total of 17,169 volunteers to Thailand, covering schools and colleges in 73 provinces.

On the other hand, the training of local Chinese language teachers is further strengthened through the training programs for research and study for the local Thai Chinese language teachers in China as well as in Thailand. In China, the Chinese Language Teacher Training Program for Bangkok Education Bureau was held in Tianjin Normal University in April of 2019, and about 20 Thai local Chinese language teachers participated in the training. In the same month, 18 teachers from Thailand North Agricultural Vocational Education College attended a one-week Chinese language and culture training in Shaanxi Energy Vocational and Technical College. In Thailand, the 2019 Training for Thai Local Chinese Language Teachers was held by the Confucius Institute at Assumption University on January 18th–19th. A total of 53 local Chinese language teachers from 41 educational institutions participated in the training. From March 25th to April 3rd, the Vocational Education Commission of the Ministry of Education of Thailand organized the 2019 Chinese Language Training for Teachers of the Vocational Education Commission of Thailand. 74 teachers of the Vocational Education Commission of Thailand from 44 provinces participated in the training. December 12th–13th, Confucius Institute at Chiang Mai University in Thailand held the "2019 North Thailand Local Chinese Language Teacher Training & Southeast Asia International Chinese Language Education Seminar (Chiang Mai)", which was attended by nearly 100 local Chinese language teachers from 10 provinces in the North of Thailand and Bangkok.

2. TCSOL in South Korea

With the prosperous economic and trade exchanges between China and South Korea, more Korean companies attach importance to Chinese language skills when recruiting, and learning Chinese language in South Korea continues to gain popularity in 2019. It is estimated that out of 50 million people in South Korea, there are more than 10.6 million people learning Chinese language and Chinese characters, the number ranking first in the world. In 2019, South Korea hosted 23 Confucius Institutes and five

Confucius Classrooms. According to Statics Korea, people learning Chinese language by various means in 2019 increased by 16.2% compared to those in 2018. Chinese language education market in South Korea in 2018 exceeded 700 billion KRW, which is about 4 billion RMB.

In 2019, Chinese language education in South Korea still focuses on learning Chinese and "Chinese +" subjects. It is especially worth mentioning that South Korea attaches great importance to the localization of Chinese textbooks and has compiled and published many Chinese textbooks. So far, Chinese textbooks produced by China and by South Korea account for half of the market share respectively. Meanwhile, sales of Chinese textbooks have risen year by year, with more than 180 types of textbooks. However, the learners there prefer local textbooks, and the best-selling Chinese textbook in 2019 is still *Delicious Chinese*, a crash oral speaking textbook compiled by the JRC Chinese Language Institute in South Korea.

In addition, the number of HSK testees continues to set new records, especially in recent years, that number has been growing by 200 per year. In 2019, the number exceeded 100,000, ranking the highest in the world.

III. Reflection on Development

"Mandarin fever" still lingers in Asia in 2019, and TCSOL has achieved great success both in policy planning and in teaching and testing. Looking ahead, we believe that:

(1) More countries will integrate Chinese language into their national education systems.

(2) The era of "Chinese +" is in full swing as the demand for Chinese language in Asia becomes more diversified and differentiated, especially in the countries along the "Belt and Road". There will be a greater demand for "Chinese + vocational skills" education.

(3) As for teacher supply, two strategies will still be adopted: sending teachers

abroad and training local teachers.

(4) Although the cultural distance among Asian countries is smaller compared to that from Western countries, in the construction of TCSOL textbooks, the principle of compiling country-specific and localized teaching materials should be adhered to, and the best way is joint compilation by China and foreign countries.

(5) With the advent of the intelligent era and mature Internet technology, the teaching modes will be more flexible and diverse. Meanwhile, in-person teaching, online teaching and hybrid/blended teaching will become the common teaching modes. Therefore, systematic teaching standards, teaching norms and so on need improving.

(Guo Fenglan, Beijing Language and Culture University)

Report on the Development of Integrating Chinese into National Education Systems in Europe — Taking the UK as an Example

The UK is one of the first Western European countries to incorporate Chinese language into its national education system. The education system in the UK consists of that of England, Scotland, Wales, and Northern Ireland. Though Chinese language is taught in some primary and secondary schools in the latter two regions, but not many, and there is no official graduation examination of Chinese language for the middle and high school students there, so this report only introduces the Chinese language education in England and Scotland.

The integration of Chinese language into the national education system in the UK has gone through three phases: (1) The first phase is official approval by introducing policies, where Chinese language as a school subject of foreign language was officially recognized in the British education system. (2) The second phase is the incorporation of Chinese language in school teaching system, where Chinese language teaching was established comprehensively, including syllabus, teacher training, and textbook development, etc., and achieved the same status as other foreign language subjects. (3) The third phase is deep integration, where the scale of Chinese language teaching was expanded; the number of learners and examinees taking Chinese language and their test scores ranked high among those of all foreign language subjects in the UK.

I. Foreign Language Policies and Chinese Language Education

Although Chinese language has been a subject of graduation examination in the middle and high schools in the UK for a long time, it has only represented as a community language for quite a while, and few mainstream schools offer Chinese language courses. Learners and examinees are mainly ethnic Chinese, most of whom attend classes in Chinese community schools on weekends. In 2002, the UK government issued *Languages for All: Languages for Life—A Strategy for England*, planning to offer foreign language education in primary schools, remove the previous requirements for foreign language exams in the graduation examination (at the age of 16) for secondary school students, and increase the quantity provision of the modern foreign languages (previously only European languages were available, and now Chinese is included), so that schools can choose languages in light of their own situation. (The graduation examinations in the middle schools in England and Scotland cover 17 languages and 9 languages respectively.) *The National Curriculum in England*, published in 2014, specified that schools only need to offer foreign language education at Key Stage 2 (7-11 years old) and Key Stage 3 (11-14 years old) out of the four stages of compulsory education. It was the policy above that encouraged Chinese language education to develop step by step and deeply integrate into the national education system in the UK. Additionally, the communication and cooperation between the Chinese and the UK governments, especially in language education, were constantly strengthened during this period, which also promoted the development and integration.

The development of Chinese language education in state primary schools in the UK is indispensable from the Confucius Classrooms, and its speed has slowed down in recent years. According to *Language Trends 2019*, most primary schools still teach European languages such as French, and less than 3% of primary schools offer Chinese language courses, similar to the situation a few years ago. A private bilingual primary school in London that was established in 2017 charges very high tuition fee and has seen an increase in the number of enrollments over the past two years: from a dozen or so in the beginning to dozens in 2019, showing a certain market demand and potential.

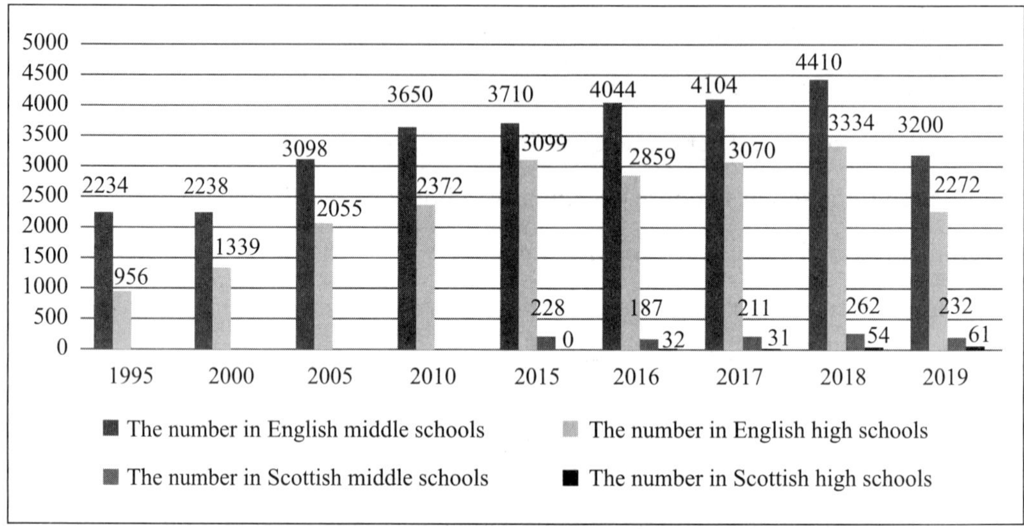

Figure 1 The Number of Students Taking the Graduation Examination in Middle and High Schools

By contrast, Chinese language education in secondary schools in the UK has developed more rapidly. In 2016, about 40% of independent secondary schools and 13% of state secondary schools offered Chinese language courses. In the same year, the Department for Education of the UK provided 10 million pounds to establish the five-year Mandarin Excellence Programme (MEP), which has played a great role in promoting Chinese language education in the state schools in recent years. Nevertheless, the development of Chinese language education in the secondary schools in 2019 had mixed gains and losses. The good news was that the number of schools offering Chinese language courses and that of students have both increased. Besides, the number of schools participating in the Programme has reached 76, and that of participating students has exceeded the target number of 5,000 for secondary school students learning Chinese language set by the Programme. The worrying thing is that, in England, the number of students taking part in the graduation examination of Chinese language in the middle schools and high schools has dropped significantly (see Figure 1), with a decrease of 27%

and 32% respectively. As a result, the graduation examination on Chinese language in the high schools lost its third place position of surpassing German in the previous year.

The Chinese language education in Scotland started relatively late: the graduation examination of Chinese language in the middle and high schools only begin in 2008 and 2010 respectively. Over the past few years, there have been fluctuations in the number of examinees participating in the graduation examination in middle schools; the number of examinees in high schools has been on the rise, but the number is still small.

II. Test Syllabus and the Graduation Examination in Secondary Schools

The syllabus of Chinese language test is an important part of the incorporation of Chinese language into the national education system in the UK. That syllabus in England has been revised several times so far. It originally set Chinese language as a community language "tailored" for ethnic Chinese students. After the foreign language policy was changed in this century, it made Chinese language an "approachable" modern foreign language that is accessible to the students of other languages and cultural backgrounds. In 2017, the syllabus was reformed again, and the year of 2019 witnessed the first implementation of the reformed syllabus. According to some teachers and students, the new syllabus is more complicated than the original one, and the difficulty of syllabuses designed by different exam boards are also different.

The main reasons for the decline of the number of students participating in the two examinations of Chinese language in 2019 may be as follows: (1) The impact of the new syllabus. Statistics from the graduation examination in high schools showed that for languages with the new syllabus, such as Chinese, Russian, and Italian, the number of examinees dropped by about 29% on average. As for the examinations in the middle schools administered by different exam boards, the number of examinees also showed a sharp drop. The number of examinees participating in the examination administered by Pearson Test of English Academic Committee fell by more than half compared with that of 2018, from 3,733 to 1,684. By contrast, the number of examinees taking examinations administered by The Assessment and Qualifications Alliance more than doubled from 710 to 1,556. (2) The competition against other foreign languages. Foreign language courses offered in secondary schools have limited teaching hours, which decreased further as a result of the increase of the quantity of foreign languages. In 2019, apart from French, German, and Spanish, the total number of students studying "other modern foreign languages" in secondary schools increased. Particularly, the number of examinees taking the tests of community languages related to the students' heritage background, such as Polish and Arabic, has increased significantly, especially in the graduation examination in high schools. (3) The factor of the younger age: the students who participated in the Programme were too young to take the graduation examination in the middle schools in 2019. More than 3,000 of them took the exam which is oriented to Key Stage 3 students (Grades 7-9) in the Programme that year, and they will gradually take the graduation examination in their middle schools in the next few years. However, there is still a big gap between the number of participants in the graduation examination of Chinese language in the middle schools and that of the three major European languages. For example, the number of examinees of Chinese language is only one-fortieth of that of French. It is difficult to change this situation in a short period of time.

Examinees taking the two graduation examinations of Chinese language still performed well in spite of the challenges of the reformed syllabus. For example, nearly 70% of middle school students who participated in the graduation examination of Chinese language administered by Pearson Test of English Academic Committee achieved A* or A. By comparison, less than 13% of students taking the French examination achieved such grades. The results of the graduation examination in high schools in 2019 showed that the examinees who achieved A* or A accounted for 25.5% of the total, a decrease of about 1% compared with that in 2018. However, nearly 36% of high school students taking the graduation examination of Chinese language administered by Pearson Test of English Academic Committee achieved such grades, which was 10 percentage points higher than the average and basically the same as that of the three major European languages. The results of Chinese language examination in Scotland also outperformed that of other language examinations considerably. However, according to some reports, among those examinees, there were many ethnic Chinese students and the Chinese students studying in the UK.

III. Teacher Training and Textbook Compilation

Teacher training and textbook compilation are also important parts of the incorporation of Chinese language into the national education system in the UK. The Thousand Talents Programme established in 2010 and the Secondary Post Graduate Certificate in Education marked the establishment of the mechanism for Chinese language teacher training. Even though there have been ups and downs in recent years, the year of 2019 saw a steady progress. The Programme aims to train 100 qualified Chinese language teachers, and UCL Institute of Education alone has enrolled more than 20. Besides, Oxford University, Manchester Metropolitan University, University of Portsmouth, Goldsmiths, University of London, University of Bolton and other universities also offer courses of Chinese language teacher certificate for secondary schools, either Chinese language alone or in conjunction with other modern foreign languages; some universities added Chinese language to their training courses of community language teachers (non-mainstream foreign languages). However, the number of local students taking those courses is still relatively low, which is influenced by admission requirements, employment opportunities, etc. Those are also the reasons why some universities (i.e., Edge Hill University) stopped enrolling students for the Chinese language teacher training programme. The Scottish government has funded Chinese language teacher training since 2007. At present, University of Aberdeen, University of Edinburgh and University of Strathclyde all offer courses for Secondary Post Graduate Diploma in Education.

The exam boards administering Chinese language exams in England have almost all developed their own middle school textbooks, such as *Jinbu* and *Edexcel GCSE Chinese* developed by Pearson as well as *AQA GCSE Chinese* (two-volume) by the Assessment and Qualifications Alliance. No single textbook is designed for the Chinese language exams in high schools, but in England, there are supplementary teaching materials every year, which are developed by Chinese language teachers and published locally. In 2019 alone, there were nearly 10 kinds of materials published, such as *Chinese for AS*. Scotland has not yet systematically developed Chinese language textbooks of their own.

In light of the degree of incorporation of Chinese language into the national education system in the UK, the Chinese language education in middle schools in the UK is still on a small scale, while the high school sector has entered the third phase. The development in 2019 had both gains and losses, but it basically remained stable. The successful implementation of the Mandarin Excellence Programme (MEP) has consolidated the position of Chinese language in the foreign language education system in the UK. Besides, more students will benefit from the accumulation of Chinese language teaching experience as well as the improvement of teaching quality over the years and continue to study Chinese language. Therefore, the number of participants in the two examinations is expected to rebound in the next few years.

In 2019, more than 300 Chinese language teachers were sent from China to the UK through the Confucius Institute Headquarters and the Chinese Language Assistant Programme of the British Council. There are hundreds of volunteer Chinese teachers working in primary and secondary schools in the UK through other channels, such as regional education exchange programmes. The UK has the largest number of Confucius Institutes and Confucius Classrooms in Europe. State schools in the UK rely on those programmes due to insufficient funding.

(Zhang Xinsheng, Richmond, the American International University in London; Li Mingfang, Regent's University London)

Report on the Development of Chinese Language Education in the Americas —Taking the United States as an Example

The world, the United States keep close ties and extensive exchanges and cooperation with China in various fields such as culture, education, science, and technology. Therefore, Chinese language education in the United States is an indispensable part of global Chinese language education. This chapter consists of seven sections, providing a general picture of Chinese language education in the US: (1) The categories of Chinese language education in the US. (2) The development of Chinese language education in American colleges and universities. (3) The development of the Confucius Institutes in the US. (4) The status of Chinese language education in the US. (5) The selection and use of Chinese language textbooks. (6) The test standards for foreign languages. (7) The main Chinese language education associations in the US. By using numbers, tables as well as examples, the author of this report will help readers understand the situation of Chinese language education in the US and provide reference for the study of Chinese language education around the world.

I. The Categories of Chinese Language Education in the US

Chinese language education provision in the US is rich in varity and is divided into the following three categories: (1) Chinese language education in American colleges and universities. (2) Chinese language education in American primary and secondary schools. (3) Chinese language education in Chinese language schools. Among them, Chinese language programs in colleges and universities are the most valued and esteemed, followed by those in primary and secondary schools and then in Chinese language schools. These three categories vary in terms of target learners, teaching methods, educational purposes, and the use of teaching materials which naturally lead to the variation of teaching effects and learning outcomes.

1. Chinese Language Education in American Colleges and Universities

In the US, many colleges and universities require students to master a foreign language by the time they graduate, usually reaching the level of their second year of the language course study. Students are required to take a placement test administered by the university at the beginning of the new semester, and those who meet the criteria above can apply for exemption from taking a foreign language course. If not, they need to take a foreign language course. For example, a freshman who has studied Chinese language in high school for four years before entering the university will be eligible to take the second-year Chinese language class after the Chinese placement test, and will need to study Chinese for at least one more year and then pass the examination before he or she can graduate. If a student enters the university with zero or preliminary Chinese language study, he or she will need to start with the first-year Chinese language class and study for two years before he or she can meet the foreign language requirements for graduation from the university. Of course, after two years of language study, this student can continue to take Chinese language courses of upper levels. So most American university students choose a foreign language, such as Chinese, as an elective course and only a small number of students study a foreign language as their major. If a student chooses to major in Chinese, he or she will be required to complete four years of Chinese language study and take a significant number of courses related to Chinese culture.

The most important feature of Chinese language education in American colleges and universities is that Chinese language is only an elective course, not a compulsory or mandatory subject. Chinese language classes are usually small, with only about 15 students. The class is a 50-minute session a day, and meets four to five times a week. Teachers generally adopts immersion language teaching methods in class, where both teachers and students speak Chinese in class, and students are guided to practice listening and speaking Chinese.

Another feature of Chinese language education in American colleges and universities is the division of Chinese heritage learners and non-Chinese heritage learners, which means these two groups of learners are placed into different classes. As ethnic Chinese students have been speaking Chinese at home with their parents since their childhood, the main goal of their classes is to learn reading and writing in Chinese. Chinese heritage learners' pace of mastering Chinese characters and the progress of their writing skills are generally twice as fast as that of non-Chinese heritage learners.

2. Chinese Language Education in American Primary and Secondary Schools

College students can choose to study a foreign language as they want, but the students in primary and secondary schools generally do not have such a choice. Based on the availability of language teachers, the school will decide on which foreign language to be taught, Chinese, Spanish, or French, and for which grade or the class. There are about 30 students each class in primary and secondary schools. Since the foreign language is not a course of their own choice, students are less motivated to learn it. So problems, such as lack both in attention and discipline, are not uncommon in most language classes. Considering these issues, Chinese teachers need to work out a realistic syllabus, adjust their teaching methods and lower the testing standards so as to maintain the students' motivation to learn Chinese. Young age is one of the salient characteristics of the students in primary and secondary schools, and they are apt to acquiring a new language, especially in pronunciation. With proper guidance, teachers can cultivate high-potential students with good pronunciation, and that will lay a solid foundation for them to improve their Chinese proficiency when they are in colleges or universities. Generally, after learning four years of Chinese language in middle schools, students can enter the second-year-level Chinese language course of universities.

3. Chinese Language Education in Chinese Language Schools

There are now four million Chinese-Americans in the United States. Many Chinese parents hope their children could learn Chinese language and keep affinity with Chinese culture as they do. So they drive their children to nearby Chinese language schools to learn Chinese language. Students in these Chinese language schools generally age from 5 to 15, an age of seeking fun while learning. They go to the Chinese schools on weekends usually not out of their own will, but at the request of their parents. They will do whatever their parents and Chinese teachers ask them to do, since Chinese children are generally more obedient. Of course, the schools and the teachers also try their best to make the Chinese courses interesting and engaging. In these Chinese language schools, the teachers use Chinese language as a tool to organize classroom games, Chinese speech and composition contests. They assign students to watch Chinese movies and TV programs, learn Chinese songs, practice martial arts, learn to play chess and so on. The teachers try their best to make the student learn Chinese language and culture through lively activities. The publishers in China have developed many teaching materials for Chinese learners at overseas Chinese language schools and produced a variety of supplementary teaching videos, which have greatly facilitated the teaching activities of the Chinese language schools in the United States.

Every summer, some Chinese language schools also organize the so-called “ancestry travels” for students and their parents to visit China. The partnership departments in China provide great assistance in this respect, allowing the Chinese heritage learners to enjoy the beautiful scenery of their ancestral country, to feel the warmth and care of their relatives in China, and to cultivate love seeds in their hearts for both Chinese language and for China.

II. The Development of Chinese Language Education in American Colleges and Universities

In the early years before 1960, the number of students learning Chinese language in the United States was not large, and there were no accurate statistical data available. The Modern Language Association (MLA) has counted the number of students taking foreign languages in American colleges and universities in the fall semester every three or four years since1960. The following chart is compiled according to the figures provided by the Modern Language Association:

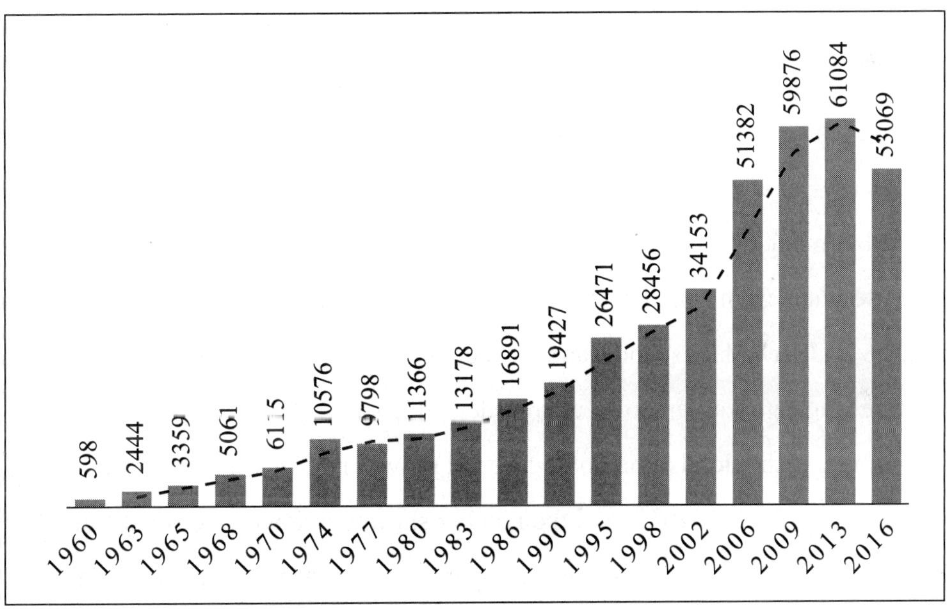

Figure 1 Numbers of American College and University Students Taking Chinese Courses in Fall Semesters, from 1960 to 2016

From the chart above, the changing trend for the number of the students learning Chinese language in American colleges and universities can be deduced and predicted. Chinese language teaching has been developing in the United States from a small to a large scale, concomitantly with the change and evolution of Sino-US relations. In 1958, the United States promulgated the *National Defense Education Act*, which listed Chinese language as one of the critical languages to national security and called on colleges and universities with resources to offer Chinese courses. At that time, there were fewer than 600 students studying Chinese. The significant events, such as the Ping-Pong diplomacy in 1971, Nixon's visit to China in 1972 and the establishment of diplomatic relations between two countries in 1979, all aroused the enthusiasm of American people to learn Chinese, and the number of the students taking Chinese language as an elective course increased significantly. China implemented the reform and opening up policy in 1978, and a large number of Chinese students studied in America. Many of those Chinese students settled down there as Chinese language teachers after completing their studies, instilling new vitality to the Chinese language teaching field in the United States. Since then, there has been a rapid growth of Chinese language learners in the United States, especially after China's economic boom in the new century. Many American students found that learning Chinese helped them find good jobs, so more students began to learn Chinese. In addition, the biggest boost to Chinese language education has been the establishment of Confucius Institutes (CIs), where a large number of Chinese language teachers from China have expanded Chinese teaching to a larger scale, reaching elementary and secondary schools and local communities, and have increased the number of Chinese language learners to an unprecedented level.

However, it should also be noted that the growth rate of Chinese learners began to slow down from 2009 to 2013, and the number showed a downward trend from 2013 to 2016. The new statistics are to be released by the MLA of America in the fall of 2021. No concrete conclusion can be drawn about the trend of the number of Chinese learners in recent years, since the number of Chinese language learners in the United States in 2021 is not available yet. To get a better understanding of the current situation, the author of this report did an investigation on some colleges and universities through WeChat groups at the end of 2020. Through summarizing and comparing the feedback provided by the classroom teachers, the author reached the following conclusions: (1) Since 2010, the number of students learning Chinese in American colleges and universities has slowed down, indicating that the peak time has passed. (2) The number of students studying

Chinese language has declined since 2013 and has continued to ebb since 2016. (3) The number of Chinese language learners leveled off in 2019 and 2020, but much lower comparing with its peak in 2010. Taking Northwestern University as an example. There were 195 students learning Chinese in the fall of 2004. Rising year by year, the number reached its peak at 368 in 2011. From then on, it fell all the way to the bottom in 2018 with 162 students. In 2019, it began to rebound and reached 222 in the fall of 2020.

Why the number of the students learning Chinese in the United States has stopped rising, or even declined? After a round of interviews with the professors at the universities, the author of this report summed up the following reasons:

(1) The number of students is reaching its saturation point. In the United States, the students who have the willingness, the need and the ability to learn Chinese language have already taken Chinese courses. When the total number reaches a certain mark, it will go stable and stop continuing to grow.

(2) The media distorts the truth. The so-called "China threat" has led some media to over-stretch the negative side of China, thus, some Americans may not choose to learn Chinese language due to their misunderstanding about China.

(3) The politicians sabotage. Some politicians have smeared and suppressed Confucius Institutes for hidden political purposes, resulting in the closure of some Confucius Institutes in the United States. The closure of Confucius Institutes and Confucius Classrooms naturally affects the development of Chinese teaching in the United States. The following section is devoted to the challenges faced by the Confucius Institutes in the United States.

III. The Development of the Confucius Institutes in the US

Since the establishment of the first Confucius Institute (CI) in the United States at the University of Maryland in 2004, CIs in the United States have developed by leaps and bounds in the years after that, from a few to 107 CIs and numerous Confucius Classrooms, which have boosted Chinese language education and the spread of Chinese culture in the United States. In the book *Chinese Teaching in America: An Analysis of Its Past, Present and Future*, the author surveys 14 Confucius Institutes in the Midwest of the United States and makes a table as follows:

Table 1 Confucius Institutes in the Midwest of the United States

Name	Establishment Time	Key Functions and Features
Confucius Institute at the University of Kansas	May, 2006	Online Chinese language teaching in secondary schools, business group training, and a series of cultural activities
Confucius Institute at Michigan State University	May, 2006	Chinese language teaching (especially online Chinese language teaching), curriculum development, teacher training and cultural exchange activities
Confucius Institute in Chicago	May, 2006	Promoting Chinese language teaching and curriculum development in 43 public primary and secondary schools, providing supplementary teaching materials and teacher training
Confucius Institute at the University of Iowa	September, 2006	Starting a series of courses, Chinese language teacher training, broadening the scope of Chinese language learning in communities, and promoting cross-cultural understanding
Confucius Institute at Purdue University	May, 2007	Offering oral Chinese and Chinese culture courses, teacher training, teaching research, translation and other consulting services
Confucius Institute at the Community College of Denver	September, 2007	Chinese language teaching, Chinese cultural activities, and carrying out a series of activities in communities
Confucius Institute at Valparaiso University	February, 2008	Carrying out Chinese language teaching and expanding Chinese language teaching market, holding Chinese music festival to introduce Chinese music and culture
Confucius Institute at Valparaiso University	April, 2008	Starting Chinese language courses, providing seminars on business disciplines and culture, and conducting Chinese language teacher certification

Name	Establishment Time	Key Functions and Features
Confucius Institute in Indianapolis	April, 2008	Carrying out Chinese language teaching, teacher training, conducting cultural exchanges in the communities, and promoting inter-school interactions
Confucius Institute at the University of Minnesota	September, 2008	Developing Chinese language teaching and proficiency testing as well as organizing cultural activities and teacher training
Confucius Institute at Webster University	February, 2009	Offering language and cultural teaching resources to promote exchanges in education and culture with China
Confucius Institute at the University of Michigan	November, 2009	Holding seminars, performances, lectures, and exhibitions on various subjects featured with the arts
Confucius Institute at Western Michigan University	November, 2009	Offering Chinese language and culture courses, compiling teaching materials, conducting teaching research, and holding cultural exchange activities
Confucius Institute at the University of Chicago	June, 2010	Carrying out research on contemporary China, especially on China's contemporary economic research

The 14 Confucius Institutes in the Midwest of the United States have their own characteristics, but they share one commitment of promoting Chinese language teaching and Chinese culture from different angles. In the past few years, Confucius Institutes have had a significant impact in the Midwest of the United States. More Americans have been exposed to Chinese culture, more students have been interested in learning Chinese, and more Americans have expressed their hope to visit China. Those important achievements of the Confucius Institutes in the United States have been witnessed by the world.

In light of the reasons mentioned above, the number of Confucius Institutes in the United States has declined significantly in recent years. It's worthy of respect that these Confucius Institutes continue with Chinese language teaching, spreading Chinese knowledge and promoting Chinese culture. Forging ahead in adversity, those Confucius Institutes are much supported by many American teachers and appreciated by the public.

IV. The Status of Chinese Language Education in the US

In the US, foreign language teaching is service-oriented, serving regional studies or professional disciplines, and Chinese language teaching is no exception. For example, students majoring in Chinese literature need to read literature works in Chinese, so they take Chinese language class to improve their reading skills and proficiency in Chinese. That is why in many universities, those who teach Chinese literature and other similar subjects are tenured professors, while those who teach Chinese language are just instructors. Although their jobs are fairly stable, the language instructors do not have tenure. As for the heads of Chinese language departments in universities, many of them are merely senior instructors without tenure, although they are also PhD holders in TCSOL (Teaching Chinese to the Speakers of Other Languages), linguistics, or pedagogy.

Generally speaking, there are no independent Chinese language departments in American colleges and universities; there are the Department of East Asian Studies, or the Department of Asian Languages and Cultures, where Chinese language is one of its language programs. In general, the status of the Department of East Asian Studies or the Department of Asian Languages and Cultures is similar to that of the Department of History or the Department of Religion, not comparable to that of the Department of Science and Technology and other hard sciences. Concerning the status of Chinese language program, there is no much difference whether it is offered in the Ivy League colleges and universities or in other state universities. For instance, the Chinese language program in Princeton University is much stronger than that in Northwestern University, but the status of the two at their own university is nearly the same. I have this knowledge because I was a faculty member of Princeton University before joining Northwestern University. It should be acknowledged that with China's rapid economic development and rising status in the international community in recent years, American colleges and universities have more interactions with Chinese universities, which have given Chinese language programs more visibility in their American universities. I hope this momentum will continue to grow.

V. The Selection and Use of Chinese Language Textbooks

There is no uniform syllabus for Chinese language education in the United States. Tailored to the actual needs of the students, the universities formulate their own syllabuses for their Chinese language programs, and choose the textbooks and teaching materials suitable for their teaching goals and objectives.

The textbooks selected by the American colleges and universities are increasingly localized. In order to know the current situation of the adoption of Chinese language textbooks in American colleges and universities, Professor Li Yu and the collaborators at Emory University conducted a questionnaire survey of 170 colleges and universities in the US and published their survey report in the *Journal of Chinese Language Teaching Research—Chinese Language Teachers Association of America*, Vol. 49, 2014. According to Professor Li Yu, the most widely used Chinese language textbooks for the junior levels in American colleges and universities are *Integrated Chinese*, and the most widely used textbooks for the senior levels are *All Things Considered*. Both sets of textbooks were written by local American Chinese language teachers. Professor Liang Xia of the University of Washington points out in her new book *Teaching Chinese in American Colleges* that the most important feature of those two sets of textbooks is their clear target readership. The textbooks are compiled for the specific grade levels in line with the length of the semesters of the university, the number of classes per week, and the scenarios of students' daily life. Professor Liang Xia holds that the compilers of those two sets of textbooks have rich teaching experience in American colleges and universities as well as a clear awareness of comparing the two grammars of English and Chinese languages and the two cultures. The perspectives, ideologies, and values presented in the texts and the discussions in these textbooks are more consistent and resonant with those of American students.

Teachers of different classes at every university in the US can choose their own preferred teaching materials. The table below from Northwestern University show the textbooks used by its Chinese language teachers:

Table 2 Chinese Courses and the Textbooks Used in Northwestern University

Course Name	Textbook
First Grade	*Modern Chinese*, 1A & 1B
Second Grade	*Modern Chinese*, 1B & 2A
Third Grade	*Developing Chinese Fluency*
Fourth Grade	*The Routledge Advanced Chinese Multimedia Course—Crossing Cultural Boundaries, Reading Short Short Stories*
Chinese Heritage Learners I	*Integrated Chinese*, Novice I & II
Chinese Heritage Learners II	*Integrated Chinese*, Intermediate I & II
Chinese Heritage Learners III	*Reading into a New China, Reading China: A Panorama of Life, Culture, and Society*
Chinese Heritage Learners IV	*Road to Success, Upper Elementary*, 1 & 2
Business Chinese	*New Silk Road*

Among the nine sets of different textbooks above, seven of them were published in the US; only two sets of textbooks—*Road to Success* and *New Silk Road* were published in China, by Beijing Language and Culture University Press and by Peking University Press respectively. The table above provides evidence supporting Professor Li's survey report in 2014 and Professor Liang's analysis in 2020. Therefore, it can be concluded that American teachers and students prefer the textbooks compiled by local American Chinese language teachers, since these textbooks, in the aspects of formats, contents, audio-visualization, as well as in after-sales service, all cater to the need of Chinese language learners in the United States.

VI. The Test Standards for Foreign Languages

ACTFL Proficiency Guidelines, formulated by American Council on the Teaching of Foreign Languages (ACTFL), marks a milestone in the standardization of foreign language teaching. The *Guidelines* describes in detail the different levels of foreign language tasks that students at different levels need to complete. Regardless the differences between different languages, the *Guidelines* sets unified standards and provides a yardstick for foreign language teaching. No matter which language family a language belongs to or how difficult it is to learn, the learning goals and plans are set based on the standards and criteria. Against the *Guidelines*, one can know what the stated objectives of certain courses are in a school, "Superior," "Advanced," or "Intermediate." In order to achieve the goals and the objectives, the school will take into consideration the curriculum design, teaching materials selection, teacher recruitment, etc. For example, the National Security Education Foundation (NSEF) has asked 12 universities with the Chinese Flagship Program to train their students to the "Superior" level according to the *Guidelines*. This "Superior" level clearly describes the foreign language tasks that students of this level can complete. Those schools have signed the agreement with NSEF that after four years of study, students will be tested against the "Superior" level standards. Those Flagship programs of the 12 universities can use the funding of NSEF to hire teachers, design their own syllabuses and courses, decide on teaching hours as well as course credits, so as to adjust their training to accommodate the students' realities. With specific standards and targets, both parties of the agreement are clear which proficiency level of Chinese language students should reach.

The *Guidelines* describes in detail the different levels of foreign language proficiency, from the top level of "Distinguished" to the lowest level of "Novice", i.e., what students at different levels can speak and write in a foreign language at a certain time, place, or situation, and what they cannot yet speak or write. The *Guidelines* does not conform to a specific teaching theory, methodology or syllabus, but only serves as a standard to measure the testee's foreign language proficiency.

The *Guidelines* assesses students' Chinese language proficiency in four main areas: speaking, writing, listening and reading, different from the familiar arrangement of the four abilities in China: listening, speaking, reading, and writing; instead, listening and reading are preceded by speaking and writing, and that is to distinguish between students' ability to "receive" and their ability to "produce". Speaking and writing are productive skills, while listening and reading are receptive skills.

The *Guidelines* divides the four areas of foreign language proficiency into five main levels and nine sub-levels. Taking speaking level as an example. The highest level is "Distinguished", followed by "Superior, Advanced, Intermediate, and Novice" levels; the latter four levels fall into three sub-levels: High, Mid and Low. To present the levels graphically, the *Guidelines* has developed the following pyramid chart:

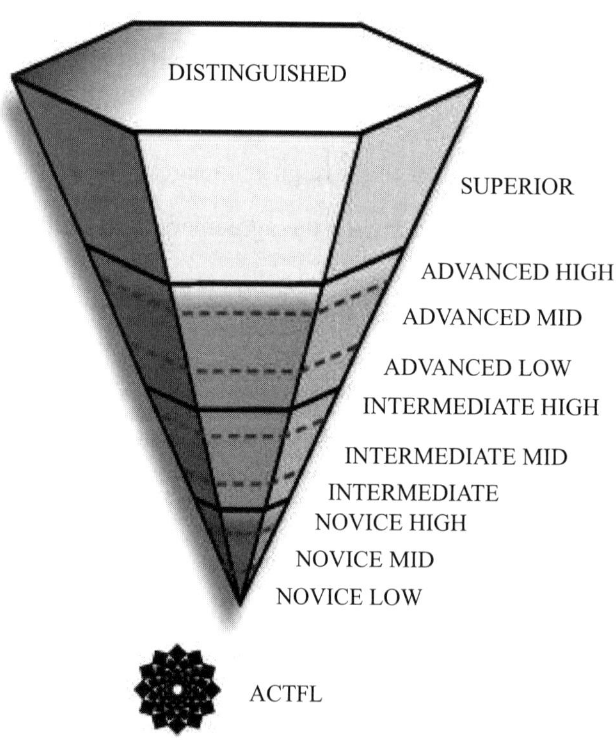

Figure 2 Schematic Diagram of Proficiency Levels in *ACTFL Proficiency Guidelines* Formulated by ACTFL

The inverted cone above represents the levels of foreign language that examinees belong to. The graph shows that students at the "Novice Low" level master the least knowledge, so they are at the bottom, in sharp contrast with the "Distinguished" level at the top. Thus, the chart above represents the amount of knowledge mastered by the students at different levels instead of the number of students at each level.

With the *Guidelines*, students can set their goals based on their actual situations no matter which school they study at or which foreign language they learn. The syllabus formulated by the Chinese Program where I work on may shed some light on this. Taking the specific circumstances of the students into consideration, we set the following goals and objectives – the students should achieve the following levels through taking different levels of Chinese courses after studying Chinese for a year:

Table 3 Chinese Language Course Target Levels

Course Title	Speaking Level	Writing Level	Listening Level	Reading Level
Chinese Language I	Novice High	Novice High	Novice High	Novice High
Chinese Language II	Intermediate Mid	Intermediate Mid	Intermediate Mid	Intermediate Low
Chinese Language III	Intermediate High	Intermediate High	Intermediate High	Intermediate Mid
Chinese Language IV	Advanced Low to Advanced Mid	Advanced Low to Advanced Mid	Advanced Low to Advanced Mid	Advanced Low to Advanced Mid
First Grade of Chinese Heritage Students	Intermediate High	Intermediate Mid to Intermediate High	Intermediate High	Intermediate Mid to Intermediate High
Second Grade of Chinese Heritage Students	Advanced Low	Intermediate High to Advanced Low	Advanced Low	Intermediate High to Advanced Low
Third Grade of Chinese Heritage Students	Advanced Mid	Advanced Low to Advanced Mid	Advanced Mid	Advanced Low to Advanced Mid
Fourth Grade of Chinese Heritage Students	Advanced High	Advanced High	Advanced High	Advanced High

Due to the different needs of Chinese heritage learners and non-Chinese heritage learners, the Chinese courses vary in terms of the time needed to reach a certain level as well as the requirements for the skills of listening, speaking, reading and writing.

VII. The Main Chinese Language Education Associations in the US

There are three major Chinese language education associations in the United States: Chinese Language Teachers Association (CLTA), Chinese Language Association of Secondary-Elementary Schools (CLASS), and Chinese School Association of the United States (CSAUS). Although they are independent organizations, they cooperate with each other.

1. Chinese Language Teachers Association (CLTA)

Chinese Language Teachers Association (CLTA) was founded in 1962. The association now has more than 700 members, who are mainly Chinese language teachers from the colleges and universities across the United States. In recent years, some primary and secondary school Chinese language teachers have also joined CLTA. The mission of the association is to promote the development and research of Chinese language teaching and Chinese culture in the US. CLTA holds an annual meeting, during which the new president is elected, and organizes thematic seminars. CLTA also publishes an academic journal *Chinese as a Second Language—The Journal of the Chinese Language Teachers Association,* three issues a year, publishing the latest outcomes of the Chinese language teaching and research. Some written in Chinese and some in English, the journal articles are subject to blind peer-review, serving as an important channel to learn about the Chinese language teaching and research in the United States. The journal emphasizes the research on teaching practice and aims to promote the development of Chinese language teaching.

2. Chinese Language Association of Secondary-Elementary Schools (CLASS)

Chinese Language Association of Secondary-Elementary Schools (CLASS) was founded in 1987. The association aims to assist primary and secondary schools in initiating and developing Chinese language programs, produce standard syllabuses, set standards for Chinese language proficiency tests, establish AP Chinese courses, and train Chinese language teachers. CLASS works closely with CLTA and holds the annual conference together. CLASS and CLTA share many members who are from either public or private K-12 schools across the United States.

3. Chinese School Association of the United States (CSAUS)

Chinese School Association of the United States (CSAUS) was founded in 1994. The association has a membership of more than 500 Chinese language schools from all 50 states. Now there are more than 100,000 Chinese language students and about 8,000 teachers. The purpose of the association is to strengthen the exchanges and cooperation among Chinese schools in the USA, promote the education of Chinese language and culture in the USA, and promote cultural exchanges and cooperation between China and the USA. CSAUS holds a conference every two years to elect a new president, discuss future visions and formulate activity plans: such as organizing students to go on "ancestral travels" to China, holding Chinese language speech contests as well as composition contests and so on. Unlike primary and secondary schools and universities, Chinese language schools only hold classes on Saturdays or Sundays, and most of them rent classrooms from secondary schools or universities. The students are primary and junior high school students, most of whom are ethnic Chinese children, with a small number of adopted children from China by American families. The purpose of CSAUS is to provide the opportunity and facility for ethnic Chinese children to learn Chinese language and maintain Chinese cultural traditions.

These three associations, i.e., CLTA, CLASS and CSAUS, serve Chinese language education in colleges and universities, in primary and secondary schools, and in Chinese language schools respectively. They serve different groups, but with the same purpose, and their work is interrelated and interlinked. For example, if Chinese language schools can stimulate Chinese children's interest in learning Chinese, primary and secondary schools will offer more Chinese courses to lay a good foundation for students, and Chinese language teaching in colleges and universities can greatly help students improve their Chinese language proficiency. Therefore, it is essential for the three associations to communicate and cooperate with each other. I am a professor at Northwestern University, and I had taught Chinese in a public high school in Chicago for four years in my spare time, and also served voluntarily as the principal of a Chinese language school for eight years, where my daughter had studied Chinese. As a member of the above three associations, I have good knowledge of them all.

In addition to the above three large associations, there are also some professional associations at the state and regional level, such as the Chinese Language Teachers Association of California (CLTAC), American Society of *Shufa* Calligraphy Education, Business Chinese Language Association, and so on. Such associations or societies have clear goals—to help Chinese language teachers enhance teaching quality and promote the development of Chinese language teaching. They organize activities, including annual meetings, president elections, Chinese language speech contests and so on.

In recent years, Chinese language education in the US has undergone rapid changes in the following aspects: educational categories, student numbers, academic status, textbook selection and compilation, test standards, organizational structures and so on. The development of Chinese language education in the United States has always benefited from the assistance from China. I believe that with the support from the Chinese partnership universities and organizations in China, Chinese language education in the US will make greater progress in the future.

(Gu Licheng, Northwestern University)

A Review of Chinese Language Education in France in 2019

The year of 2019 marks the 55th anniversary of the establishment of diplomatic relations between China and France. This is an important and extraordinary year for the peoples of the two countries in diplomacy. At the same time, it is also a year of great significance in Chinese language education in France. It is known to all that the past fifteen years has witnessed a gratifying phenomenon in France where more and more people are studying Chinese. This good trend continues in 2019. According to the latest statistics available, the number of people who have studied Chinese language in France has reached more than 100,000[1]. Furthermore, France has more people taking Chinese proficiency test (HSK) than any other country in Europe.

This report will first examine the situation of Chinese language teaching at different educational levels in France in 2019, then it will introduce the development of Chinese language teaching in other fields in France.

I. The Situation of Chinese Language Teaching at Different Educational Levels in France

1. Chinese Language Teaching in Primary Schools

The number of primary school students learning Chinese in France reached more than 6,000 in 2019. There are now 70 primary schools in France that offer Chinese

1 See Joël Bellassen (2016). The general report on Chinese language teaching was no longer published after General Inspector Joël Bellassen's term.

language courses[1]. Those schools fall into three types: primary schools in France, schools overseas and international classes in primary schools. Generally speaking, French pupils begin to learn foreign languages in pre-primary schools. Some children are lucky enough to be taught Chinese from kindergarten so that they can start to communicate in Chinese from then, such as the children at the French-Chinese kindergarten in Paris and Montessori kid's home[2]. In foreign language teaching, primary school teachers attach great importance to arousing children's sense of language. In France, most students used to study English, but now more and more children choose Chinese. Chinese becomes their second foreign language. As early as 2002, the French Ministry of National Education issued a Chinese language teaching syllabus for primary schools. Apart from that, there are 15 international classes in French primary schools[3], which admit both Chinese and French students. The students study and play together in school, communicating in both Chinese and French and helping each other to make progress in both languages. They are required to take Chinese language lessons three hours per week so that French students can quickly improve their Chinese in such an environment, and Chinese students can adapt to the French education system in a short time.

2. Chinese Language Teaching in Secondary Schools

It is an indisputable fact that France has played a pioneering role in the development of Chinese language teaching in secondary schools. Before the establishment of diplomatic relations between France and China, the first Chinese language course in secondary schools was set up in Paris in 1958[4]. Joël Bellassen, Inspector General in the field of Chinese Language Teaching at the French Ministry of National Education from 2006 to 2016, has made great contributions to the development of Chinese language teaching in France. He attaches great importance to promoting Chinese language education in secondary schools. He has built a complete syllabus and trained a number

1 https://www.afpc.asso.fr/Carte-du-Chinois

2 Ibid.

3 https://www.education.gouv.fr/les-sections-internationales-l-ecole-primaire-12443

4 See Joël Bellassen (2016).

of Chinese language teachers. Compared with other European countries, his practice has been recognized as a major feature of Chinese language teaching in Europe. With the guidance of the French Ministry of National Education, the efforts of local Chinese language teachers in France and Chinese language teachers sent by Chinese government, it is no exaggeration to say that there is a place to learn Chinese in everywhere of France, from the French mainland, to Corsica, to the overseas provinces and territories, plus the Confucius Institutes cooperated by China and France.

In 2019, another 51 secondary schools opened Chinese language classes[1]. The number of secondary schools (middle and high schools) offering Chinese language courses in France has reached 1,079 in 2019, a fivefold increase in the number in 2005. We should not leave out its overseas 40 French secondary schools abroad and the 28 international classes. According to the recent statistics, of the 334 middle schools that offer Chinese language courses[2], the majority (304 schools) set Chinese as a second foreign language. Chinese language teaching in French secondary schools has a good continuity of teaching and learning. 68% students who have started to learn Chinese in the middle school can continue their learning in the high school[3]. According to Bellassen (2016), half of the students study Chinese as their second foreign language[4]. 60% of high schools in France now offer courses with Chinese as a third foreign language, half of which offer Chinese language as a second and a third foreign language. Alongside the "Mandarin fever" and the importance attached to Chinese language, and the enhancement of parents' recognition and students' interest, in recent years, more than 30 middle schools have Chinese as the first foreign language; the status of Chinese language varies in the 14 high schools: in the same school, students can choose Chinese language either as their first, or as their second or third foreign language, but Chinese language is always given priority in international classes and oriental language classes. This is a regulation of the French Ministry of

1 https://fcae.fr/pdf/Lettre-N40-Mars-2020.pdf

2 http://www.onisep.fr/Choisir-mes-etudes/College/Classes-du-college/Etudier-les-langues-au-college/La-carte-des-principales-langues-vivantes-etrangeres-enseignees-pres-de-chez-vous

3 https://www.letudiant.fr/etudes/annuaire-des-lycees/langue-chinois/page-25.html

4 See Joël Bellassen (2016).

National Education, accoding to which in addition to language classes (three to five hours per week), students of international classes are also required to study other non-linguistic subjects in Chinese, such as literature, mathematics, history, and geography. Upon graduation, their diploma will specifically be noted with the "international class" or the "oriental language class"[1]. With the enhancement of scientific, technological, and cultural exchanges between France and China, and the continuous development of friendship between the two peoples, more and more people have a good understanding of China and Chinese language, now even secondary technical school students are increasingly interested in Chinese language, and the number of students increases year by year. Learning Chinese language is considered an advantage for them in their job hunting after graduation. To meet the demand of the labor market, high schools of tourism and hotel management and schools of applied arts also offer Chinese language classes[2].

In recent years, more and more teachers have been recruited as a result of the development of Chinese language teaching. Most local Chinese language teachers are not the graduates from normal universities, so there is an urgent need for professional training. Teachers from China especially need to be localized[3] to get familar with and master the teaching ideas and methods of France. In view of the urgent need for teacher training, in the summer of 2019, the French Association of Chinese Teachers (Association Francaise des Professeurs de Chinois, AFPC for short) and Northwest University (in Xi'an, China), jointly organized a three-week training course for French Chinese language teachers for the first time and won a great success. It had been well received by French Ministry of National Education and the trained teachers. To ensure the quality of Chinese language teaching, excellent teachers are indispensable. The French Ministry of National Education holds Chinese Language Teacher Qualification Examination (both internal and external) annually. In 2019, many prospective Chinese language teachers registered for the exam, 161 took the exam, but only 19 passed the exam and got the job

1 https://www.education.gouv.fr/les-sections-internationales-au-lycee-2606

2 An ongoing investigation by the French Chinese Language Teaching Association.

3 The characteristics and identity of the members of French Chinese Language Teaching Association clearly indicate this tendency.

offer[1]. There were also 51 registered internal examination for College Chinese Language Teacher Certificate, but only 39 took the exam in 2019[2]. All these show that to ensure the quality of Chinese teaching, the French Ministry of National Education has made great efforts in the construction of Chinese teaching staff by organizing more strict examinations and recruitment of Chinese language teachers.

We have entered the digital age, so have the Chinese language teaching in France. For instance, recent media reported that a Chinese language teacher at a junior high school near Toure taught students face to face in the classroom, and she also shared with junior high school students in a small rural village via video conference, and that was for the first time in France[3].

3. Chinese Language Teaching in Colleges and Universities

According to a survey by AFPC, there are more than 25,000 students studying Chinese in French colleges and universities. 52 colleges and universities offer Chinese language courses, 36 of which have Chinese language departments or offer specialized Chinese language courses, and 27 offer general Chinese language courses. Specialized courses fall into two types: applied foreign languages and foreign languages as well as literature and culture, and the department of applied foreign languages has attracted an increasing number of college students to enroll in its Chinese language courses these years. Overall, more than 18,000 students are currently studying Chinese in French colleges and universities, which should also include more than 7,000 students who spend two years preparing for the Certificate of Advanced Technologists (Brevet de Technicien Supérieur, BTS in short) and Preparatory Courses in Liberal Arts (Classes Préparatoires aux Grandes Écoles, CPGE in short)[4]. The total number has reached more than 25,000. In 2019, many colleges and universities also began to offer Chinese language courses. For example, the University of Orléans has established the Department of Applied Chinese Language.

1 https://www.devenirenseignant.gouv.fr/cid141810/donnees-statistiques-capes-2019.html

2 https://www.devenirenseignant.gouv.fr/cid143407/donnees-statistiques-agregation-2019.html

3 https://www.franceinter.fr/emissions/le-zoom-de-la-redaction/le-zoom-de-la-redaction-26-fevrier-2019

4 It is based on the statistics of the French Ministry of National Education.

No syllabus is the characteristic of Chinese language teaching in French colleges and universities. Because the French Constitution gives every university teacher the freedom to teach. The current problem facing universities is that the Chinese language teaching in universities and secondary schools are not well aligned. The number of students who now begin to study Chinese in secondary schools is increasing, and Chinese language departments in colleges and universities will inevitably have to adapt to this dramatic change. Teaching reform is needed to make Chinese language teaching suited to the needs of new university students who have learned Chinese for many years.

On June 8, 2019, AFPC held HSK tests in Paris and the second large-scale Chinese University Exhibition at the National Institute for Oriental Languages and Civilizations. Over 10 well-known Chinese universities attended the exhibition (Tsinghua University, Peking University, Beijing Normal University, University of Science and Technology Beijing, Shanghai Jiao Tong University, Northeast Normal University, Northeastern University, Zhongnan University of Economics and Law, Central China Normal University, Xidian University, Shenzhen University, Tongji University), and HSK Global Innovation Internship Project. They presented the elegant demeanor of Chinese universities and introduced their educational achievements to the general public of France, especially the university students in Paris. The exhibition attracted huge crowds of people, and was well received by the French public.

In addition to the situation mentioned above, Chinese language teaching has also made some progress in other fields in France.

II. Important Events for the Further Development of Chinese Language Teaching in 2019

1. Three Seminars on Chinese Language Teaching and Research

AFPC[1] has organized many Chinese language teaching seminars independently or together with other institutions. The conference in 2019, for example, included a

1 The thematic seminar on Chinese language teaching is organized annually.

seminar on Chinese literature and Chinese language teaching. Professor Bellassen and Jin Siyan, Professor of Artois University and Director of the Confucius Institute, delivered the keynote speeches. The seminar was presided over by Yin Wenying, Regional Inspector of French Ministry of National Education for Chinese Language Education in the Bordeaux District. The association made the point of inviting two Chinese writers, Shen Fuyu and Shucai[1] to give keynote speeches at the seminar. Apart from Chinese writers, the association also invited well-known French Sinologists and translators (Noël Dutrait, Honorary Professor Emeritus at Aix-Marseille University, and Brigitte Guilbaud, French Regional Inspector for Chinese Language Education) to share their research findings and teaching experience in Chinese language with the members of the association. In the seminar, quite a few Chinese language teachers raised some questions which need further joint research. The conference was full of academic atmosphere. On April 12th-13th, the European Association for Chinese Teaching held the 2nd International Symposium of the European Association of Chinese Teaching (EACT) in Dublin, themed "Pushing Forward the Discipline of Chinese as a Second Language—European Efforts in the World Context". The symposium was a huge success, attended by more than 200 experts and Chinese language teachers from more than 20 European countries. From June 27th to 29th, 2019, at the Artois University and its Confucius Institute, Professor Jin Siyan organized the International Symposium & the 12th Training Class on Chinese language teachers for the European Confucius Institutes and local teachers: "Monism or Duality—Chinese Language Nature and the Critical Choice of Chinese Teaching". Besides Professor Joël Bellassen, the speakers also included Zhang Xinsheng from the University of London, Zhang Hong from the University of Rome, Grâce Poizat from the Confucius Institute at the University of Geneva, and Yin Wenying, the Inspector of French Ministry of National Education for Chinese Language Education in the Bordeaux District. Chinese language teachers who participated in the symposium were much inspired and benefited a lot from the training,

1 https://www.falanxi360.com/index.php?s=/news/show/id/3343

which will play an effective role in improving Chinese language teaching capacity and level in the future.[1]

2. New Progress of the Confucius Institutes in France

Three new Confucius Institutes were established in France in 2019. The French partners were the city of Pau in southwestern France, Hautes Etudes Commerciales (HEC Paris), and the University of Orléans. As of the end of 2019, Chinese and French colleges and universities have jointly established 17 Confucius Institutes[2]. These Confucius Institutes fall into two types: the first is structured into a university, and the second type is a civil society by law. The Confucius Institutes connect people and maintain rapport with various groups, such as students, teachers, civil servants, entrepreneurs, businessmen, doctors, sailors and retirees. Confucius Institutes serve as a window into China's diverse cultures. In addition to carrying out Chinese language education and organizing HSK tests, there are a variety of Chinese cultural activities, such as Chinese film week, traditional Chinese culture exhibitions, lectures, concerts, seminars, calligraphy training classes, cooking training classes, *taijiquan* training classes, etc., which attract more and more French attendees and viewers. Of course, some Confucius Institutes enjoy their own special characteristics: some focus on the culture, some more economy-oriented, and others more business-oriented. According to their founding purpose, Confucius Institutes are non-profit organizations that promote Chinese language teaching. They also serve as the center for Chinese language tests and the consulting center for information of Chinese universities and national scholarships, accessible for students who wish to study in China. The establishment of Confucius Institutes has once again fully demonstrated the importance of China-France cooperation in cultural exchanges between the two countries. It will help strengthen the friendly relations between the French and the Chinese people and promote further cultural exchanges between the two countries.

The year of 2019 saw a thriving development of China-France cultural exchange.

---

1 http://www.oushinet.com/wap/qj/qjnews/20190501/320144 & html & http://www.ouhanhui.eu/?p=874&lang=zh

2 http://www.confucius-clermont-auvergne.org

The Confucius Institutes in France held the 2nd Chinese Literature Translation Competition, requiring the translation of the short stories by 5 Chinese writers, namely Mo Yan, Chen Lijiao, Qin Delong, Duola, Ling Dingnian[1]. In the autumn, the famous Chinese cartoonist, Li Kunwu, visited France, and the Confucius Institutes in Rennes and Clermont-Ferrand organized his special exhibitions, lectures and other activities, which were well received by the French public and students[2]. When the Confucius Institute of La Rochelle held its Chinese Film Week in the first week of October, Chinese writer and director Dai Sijie attended the festival to introduce a film called *Balzac and the Little Chinese Seamstress*, which attracted a wide audience, especially college students studying Chinese.

At the end of 2019, the International Conference on Chinese Language Education was held in Changsha, China. The Chinese and French directors of Confucius Institutes in France and many well-known Chinese language experts from around the world attended the conference and witnessed the establishment of the Chinese International Education Foundation. The reform of Hanban marked a milestone for the cause of international Chinese language education.

3. The Large-Scale Chinese Character Festival

The 2nd Paris Chinese Character Festival was launched in October 2019. A series of activities related to Chinese character culture, including exhibitions, lectures, and cultural experiences and exchanges, were held during the five-day Chinese Character Festival[3].

Chinese language education in France has experienced a new development in 2019. With the new challenges brought by digitalization, the forms of Chinese language teaching have also changed. In terms of Chinese language research and teaching, we still have much work to do. The Chinese language teaching community in France must strengthen the cooperation between local French teachers and Chinese teachers

1 https://www.institutconfucius.fr/fr/culture/concours-de-traduction

2 https://www.confucius-bretagne.org/project/li-kunwu-23-11-2019/ & https://www.rendezvous-carnetdevoyage.com/2019/10/institut-confucius/

3 See La Lettre de L'AFPC n °144

to enhance academic exchanges and cooperation with the high achievers of Chinese universities (Beijing Normal University, Beijing Language and Culture University, for instance) in Chinese language teaching through organizing short-term training courses for Chinese language teachers and international seminars on Chinese language teaching. Although the Chinese language teaching in France has achieved remarkable results, there is no doubt that it will face many challenges in the new era. Through the cooperation with Chinese universities, we believe that the teaching of Chinese language in France will make great achievements.

(Martine Raibaud, Associate Professor of La Rochelle University, French Director of the Confucius Institute at La Rochelle University, Vice President of French Chinese Language Teaching Association)

Reference: /

Bellassen, J. (2016) *Le chinois, langue* émergente, Etat de l'enseignement du chinois en 2015–2016.

IV Specialized Theme Report

Language Cognition and Second Language Acquisition

Cognition is the process and activity of brain and nervous system to shape the mind, and language is at its core. Cognitive science was established in the 1970s in the United States. At present, there are six underpinning disciplines in cognitive science recognized internationally: philosophy, linguistics, psychology, anthropology, computer science and neuroscience (Cai, 2020). As an important part of cognitive science research, the linguistic cognition research involves relevant disciplines such as linguistics, cognitive psychology, computer science and cognitive neuroscience, thus characterized by interdisciplinary integration of humanities and sciences.

Second language acquisition (SLA) is an independent research field whose core is the research on the process and the mechanism of language acquisition. Influenced by the interdisciplinary nature of linguistic cognition, SLA mainly includes three different cognitive perspectives: information processing of SLA, connectionist perspective, cognitive neuroscience, so as to explore and research the acquisition, cognition and brain neural mechanisms of second language learners, bilingual and multilingual speakers.

1. The Perspective of Information Processing in SLA

According to information processing theory, learners' language competence includes declarative knowledge and procedural knowledge. The acquisition of skills is an automatic process from declarative knowledge to procedural knowledge. In other words, learners realize the transformation from consciously controlled processing to unconsciously automatic processing in language learning or training. In recent years, the introduction of information processing theory has brought about a "cognitive turn" in the research paradigms for Chinese as a second language (CSL) acquisition. This turn has changed the research paradigm of the acquisition of habit of speech acts within the framework of behaviorist learning theory. Research on Chinese language acquisition no longer just focuses on the changes in the external speech behavior of Chinese language learners, but focuses on their internal cognitive processing mechanism (Wang, 2020).

Wei (2017) examined the chunking processing mechanism of spoken Chinese as a second language from the standpoint of cognitive processing to detect the existence or the amount of attention resources consumption. The results show that Chinese language learners' syntactic computation of phrases is carried out in a way of controlled processing. They cannot employ the way of chunking processing like native Chinese speakers do but combine multiple chunks, and that consumes attention resources and uses declarative knowledge. Through repetitive training, Chinese language learners consume less and less attention resources in syntactic computation and gradually shift to use procedural knowledge to carry out word combination within phrases. Hu and Wang (2017) focused on exploring the predictors of the spoken ability of Chinese as a second language. They selected the two indicators of cognitive fluency—the reaction time of sentence processing and the consumption of attention shift, as well as two indicators of performance fluency—speaking speed and the average length of speech flow. They used the hierarchical regression analysis to investigate the predictive effect of the two types of indicators on spoken Chinese ability. The results show that cognitive fluency can effectively improve the predictive power of spoken Chinese ability, and has a greater predictive contribution than what performance fluency does.

2. The Connectionist Perspective in SLA

The distributed representation of knowledge and parallel processing are the basic ideas of connectionism theory. The research on language acquisition under that theoretical framework mainly simulates distributed cognitive processing of the human brain through artificial neural network, so as to explore the mechanism of language knowledge representation and parallel processing of second language or bilingual learners. The research in this field casts light on and promotes the machine learning and artificial intelligence research.

Under the framework of connectionism theory, many cognitive simulation studies have been carried out both at home and abroad. In the research of SLA, Wang (2005) combined the standard self-organizing model and attention model to simulate the development of foreign students' consciousness of Chinese characters' configuration, and then explored the mechanism of CSL learners' acquisition of Chinese characters. In the area of children's vocabulary learning, Li et al. (2007) pioneered the simulation research on the "eruption" of children's vocabulary acquisition. Their research applies a self-organizing artificial neural network of "unsupervised learning" to simulate the process of children's vocabulary acquisition, and then uses the network to simulate the process of children's bilingual vocabulary acquisition. The research on simulation of Chinese phonetic acquisition of foreign learners is another field in which artificial neural networks are used for cognitive simulation. The research in that field focuses on simulating foreign learners' Chinese phonetic acquisition, the difficulties they meet in learning Chinese tones, and their acquisition mechanisms. For example, Chen (2011) used the "growing tree model" to simulate the intonation acquisition of foreign learners, and Lu (2011) used the improved self-organizing model to simulate the acquisition process and compensation mechanism of foreign learners in terms of their intonation acquisition. Those studies can make up for the deficiency of behavioral experiment and have certain advantages in exploring learners' instant processing and complex acquisition process.

3. The Perspective of Cognitive Neuroscience in SLA

Brain research is one of the most advanced scientific fields in the 21st century, and China is launching the "China Brain Project", which puts forward the strategy of "one body, two wings". The "one body" refers to the understanding of the neural basis of human cognition, which is a universal goal in neuroscience and is at the core of the strategy; the "two wings" refer to the development of the diagnosis and intervention of brain diseases as well as brain-intelligence technology, which shed light on the application for the "one body" (Poo et al., 2016). Language is the most fundamental mark to distinguish human beings from other animals. Linguistic competence is the most advanced function of human brain, which makes the research on language acquisition from the perspective of cognitive neuroscience become an important subject in the forefront of brain science research, and also an important foundation for the research and development of artificial intelligence technology (Chen, 2017). We should integrate cognitive neuroscience into language acquisition research to research second language learning, bilingual and multilingual acquisition from the perspective of cognitive neuroscience. Cognitive neuroscience is the next frontier in language acquisition research.

In 2005, *Science* proposed 125 unsolved scientific problems in the world, one of which is about the critical period of language acquisition. The neuroscience technology can reveal the cognitive neural mechanism after the critical period of language acquisition, which can make breakthroughs in the research on the bottleneck of language acquisition, thereby tackling major theoretical issues in the international academic frontier. In addition, how human brain represents and learns the form, sound and meaning of Chinese characters and words has always been the focus of researchers in the field. Syntax acquisition involves the analysis and construction of sentence components and hierarchical structure, as well as how human brain analyzes and integrates the semantic, syntactic and pragmatic information of words in a sentence. The research on those problems will reveal the nature of human language acquisition and promote the development of natural language processing in the computer. Besides, the research on second language processing and language shift can deepen the understanding of the neural correlates controlled by language processing and execution. The hypothesis of adaptation and assimilation has been proposed to explain the interaction between the brain mechanism of second language processing and that of mother tongue processing. The combination of SLA and cognitive neuroscience opens up a new field for language acquisition research and broadens its horizon.

Over the last decade or so, the research direction of CSL acquisition has shifted from structuralist linguistics to cognitive linguistics. That means the research of CSL acquisition is no longer restricted to describe learners' language structures and to analyze their errors; instead, the research on Chinese language acquisition based on language cognition will gradually become the mainstream. Although the current research on CSL acquisition is still based on the information processing theory, the emergence of new cognitive theories will broaden theoretical horizons and open up new fields for the research on CSL acquisition, such as connectionism, emergentism and cognitive neuroscience (Wang, 2020).

In order to achieve that goal, the introduction of new theories, especially interdisciplinary theories should be accelerated in the research on Chinese language acquisition based on the perspective of language cognition. In that case, we will be able to continue to broaden theoretical horizon, gradually change the previous way of emphasizing structure over cognition, and constantly expand the research field of CSL acquisition. Moreover, the exploration of research methods should be enhanced in the research on Chinese language acquisition from the perspective of language cognition. As the saying goes, "one must first sharpen his tools if he is to do his work well". The improvement of methods will considerably enhance the quality of the research on CSL acquisition and gradually reach the advanced level of the research on second language acquisition in the world. Finally, the research on the cognitive acquisition of CSL should focus on interdisciplinary research, such as cognitive neuroscience, neurolinguistics and other disciplines. Interdisciplinary research can not only promote the learning of theories, but also strengthen the modernization of research methods and means. The development of cognitive neuroscience and other research fields will certainly bring new leaps and advances to the research on Chinese language acquisition based on the perspective of language cognition (Wang, 2020).

Reference: /

Cai Shushan [蔡曙山] (2020) Lun yuyan zai renlei renzhi zhong de diwei he zuoyong (On the status and functions of language in the cognition of human beings). *Journal of Peking University: Philosophy and Social Sciences* Vol.1, 138-149.

Chen Lin [陈霖] (2017) Renzhi kexue de sandajishi (Three cornerstones of cognitive science). *Bulletin of National Natural Science Foundation of China*. No.3, 209-210.

Chen Mo [陈默] (2011) Hanyu zuowei di'er yuyan de shengdiao renzhi fazhan moni (Simulating Mandarin tone acquisition by CSL learners). *Tsinghua University* (*Science & Technology*) No. 9, 1201-1204.

Hu Weijie & Wang Jianqin [胡伟杰、王建勤] (2017) Di'er yuyan kouyu renzhi liulixing dui kouyu nengli de yuce zuoyong (Predictive power of L2 oral cognitive fluency to L2 oral competence). *Chinese Teaching in the World.* No.1, 105-115.

Lu Ji [鲁骥] (2011) Taiguo xuexizhe hanyu shengdiao fanchou xide guocheng de moni yanjiu (Simulating studies of Thailand learners in Chinese tones acquisition). PhD Thesis of Beijing Language and Culture University.

Wang Jianqin [王建勤] (2020) Jiyu renzhi shijiao de di'er yuyan xide yanjiu (*Researches on SLA from the Perspective of Cognition*). Beijing: The Commercial Press.

Wang Jianqin [王建勤] (2005) Waiguo xuesheng hanzi gouxing yishi fazhan moni yanjiu: Jiyu zizuzhi tezheng yingshe wangluo de hanzi xide moxing (Simulating studies of CFL learners' Chinese orthographic awareness development based on self-organizing feature map network). *Applied Linguistics*, No.4.

Wei Yanjun [魏岩军] (2017) Hanyu xuexizhe duoci duanyu de zukuaishi jiagong (Chunking process of multiword expressions for Chinese language learners). PhD Thesis of Beijing Language and Culture University.

Li, P., Zhao, X., & MacWhinney, B. (2007) Dynamic self-organization and early lexical development in children. *Cognitive Science,* 31, 581-612.

Poo, M. M., Du, J. L., Ip, N., Xiong, Z. Q., Xu, B., & Tan, T. (2016) China brain project: Basic neuroscience, brain diseases, and brain-inspired computing. *Neuron,* 92(3), 591-596.